GOD'S EXISTENCE:

TRUTH OR FICTION? THE ANSWER REVEALED

BY

GARY R. LINDBERG

DORRANCE
PUBLISHING CO
EST. 1920
PITTSBURGH, PENNSYLVANIA 15238

Dorrance Publishing Co
585 Alpha Drive
Pittsburgh, PA 15238
Visit our website at *www.dorrancebookstore.com*

ISBN: 978-1-6480-4273-7
eISBN: 978-1-6470-2611-0

CONTENTS

CHAPTER 1

Introduction

"The more you learn, the more you know how little you know."

— Anonymous

This is a study to explore the existence of God. Is He real or is it a fictional concept that so many people believe in? To answer the question, this study will explore botany, the human body, astronomy, mathematics, chemistry, and physics. It will also delve into the issue of Creationism versus science and review some history. The aim of this exploration is to answer the main aforementioned question. The answer may be more clear than many people realize and even much simpler than many people believe.

We humans want to make sense of the world around us and how we fit in. Since the dawn of time, humankind has asked about the nature of the world and how it came into being. What are we on this earth for? What is the purpose of our lives? These are questions we ask over and over again. One of the devices humankind has created to help answer these questions is to create gods.

Humankind has had a need for a variety of gods to exist to be able to explain things that humans could not understand and could not explain rationally. Humankind needed to better understand how and why things happened to them. It thus gave them a sense of safety and security to be able to explain phenomena that they could not otherwise explain to themselves or to others. In Ancient Greece, for example, the Greeks had many gods, but the most significant were the Olympian gods who lived majestically on Mount Olympus. The leader of the Olympian gods was Zeus. Other well-known gods included Aphrodite, Apollo, Ares, Athena, Demeter, Dionysus, Hades, Hera, Hermes, and Poseidon. These gods helped the ancient Greeks to understand the origins and nature of the world, plus the origins and significance of their own existence and ritual practices. Some of the oldest known Greek literary sources about the Greek gods were Homer's epic poems *Iliad* and *Odyssey*. He wrote other works that contain accounts about the origins of the world and other significant historical events to help the Greeks know where they came from and more about their life. Other writers added more information to increase the knowledge of the ancient Greeks.

The Romans also had many gods and most prominently included Jupiter, the chief god, Apollo, Ceres, Diana, Juno, Mars, Mercury, Minerva, Neptune, Venus, Vesta, and Vulcan. Many people are familiar with the names of the Roman gods just as they are familiar with the Greek gods. In general, the gods performed the same function for the Romans that the Greek gods did for the Greeks. These gods gave the Romans a greater sense of safety and security and understanding of the world around them in the same way as the Greek gods did for the Greeks.

A third example demonstrated this same phenomenon for the Vikings, the people from Northern Europe. Their male gods had names like Baldur, Heimdall, Loki, Njord, Odin, Thor, and Tyr. Their female gods had names like Freya, Hel, Skadi, and Sif. The Vikings also had powerful creatures that influenced people's lives, including Fenrir Wolf, Jormungandr, the Jotun, the Kraken, Odin's Ravens, and the Valkyries. These gods and creatures helped people to understand and justify strange events and forces that affected them, even though most people today are not as familiar with them as they are with the Greek and Roman gods.

Less sophisticated people had their superstitions, too, to better understand their existence as well. Witch doctors were powerful elements in their respective societies, for example, in Africa. Few dared to question what they said. That gave people order and stability in those societies.

When we examine Abraham Maslow's "Hierarchy of Needs" theory, we begin to understand where this need comes from to understand our human surroundings, origin, and history. Dr. Abraham Maslow, who was a psychologist at Brandeis University, theorized that humans are perpetually wanting animals, who always have personal needs from birth to death and who strive to fulfill their current needs according to their importance in a hierarchy of categories. These five levels of needs consist of physiological, safety, social, ego, and self-fulfillment needs. While these categories of needs remain interdependent and overlapping, the lower needs dominate the individual until they are satisfied. Then new and higher needs emerge; this process continues to the highest need of self-fulfillment that is also called self-actualization.

The most fundamental human need is physiological, such as air, food, and shelter. This need of survival or self-preservation ranks as humankind's most important motivator of behavior, according to Maslow. When this need becomes satisfied, it loses potency as a motivator. Subsequently, a person feels the need for safety, which is protection from such things as danger, threat, discrimination, and favoritism. After a person is confident that he or she will not suffer unjust and unpredictable actions by superiors or other powerful people, that person's most felt need changes to social needs. Social needs are like a desire to "belong" and to "be part of the group." Social needs also include the desire to have friends, to help others, and to be helped.

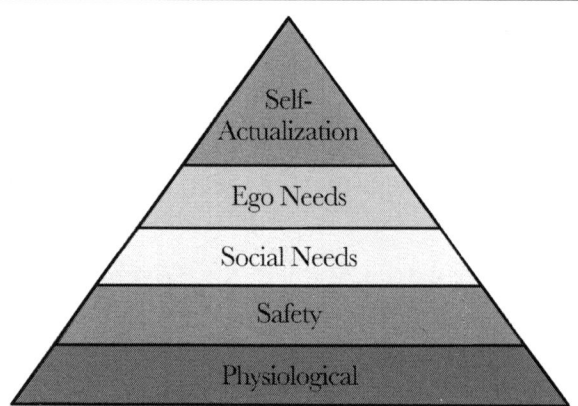

Maslow presented his theory as displayed here from Wikipedia, although our illustration uses the original words by Maslow.

Next in the hierarchy of needs stand ego needs. These are those needs that make a person able to feel comfortable with himself or herself and include self-respect, status, recognition or honor, and relative superiority in something worthwhile in the world. If ego needs become reasonably satisfied, the self-fulfillment or self-actualization needs emerge as determinants of behavior of an individual. These constitute those needs to develop himself or herself into that which he or she is capable of becoming. These needs depend on the previous satisfaction of the physiological, safety, social, and ego needs.[1]

It is possible to see from Abraham Maslow's work why people in ancient Greece, Rome, and elsewhere as well as people in our current time had, and have, a need to believe in something higher than themselves to explain certain things or forces that cannot be explained in any other way.

Now it's appropriate to discuss certain key points as we explore areas of interest in our quest to answer the main question. We will look at evidence that is available to us in many forms.

CHAPTER 2

A Look at Science

Does God exist? Many people deny the existence of God because they claim there is no physical proof of His existence. Many other people want to know whether or not that is true. Let's explore science in some detail as we start to evaluate this belief more closely. Perhaps the first question we should ask ourselves is whether or not we believe in science. Is science truthful? Is it accurate? Most of us will admit science is basically true, to the limit of our knowledge. Few of us will doubt science because there is no other body of knowledge that informs us so definitively. Science consists of many fields of knowledge. Every area of science is quite organized and very complex. Let's take a look at several areas of science. Examining botany and biology, human anatomy, and astronomy should help us to understand how science contributes to answering our main question about whether or not God exists.

Botany (and Biology)

Biology is the study of livings things and their vital processes. A look at botany is enlightening to consider. Botany is a branch of biology that focuses on the study of plants, including their structure, properties, and biochemical processes. The study of plant classification and plant diseases is also part of botany. Plants are classified in a number of levels of organization and are as follows:

Kingdom

Phylum

Class

Order

Family

Genus

Species

The list above shows the highest level or category of plant organization down to the most specific level.

This demonstrates a high amount of organization of all plant life. It's important to remember that all the plants in a particular group level share certain characteristics.

The branch of biology that studies animals is called zoology. Wikipedia defines zoology as "the branch of biology that studies the animal kingdom including the structure, embryology, evolution, classification, habits and distribution of all animals…" The aforementioned levels of organization in botany are similarly used to identify all animal life. For example, Wikipedia informs us that there are forty recognized animal phyla (the plural form of phylum). So, it is remarkable that animals are also highly systemized in terms of levels of organization. If we ponder these levels of organization, we can understand this means that all plant and animal life is extremely organized.

The Human Body

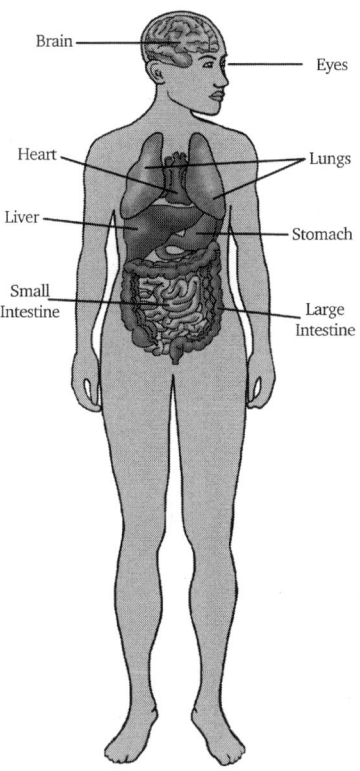

When we look at a human body, we find a very intricate, well-organized organism that functions in remarkable ways. While the human body may have as many as seventy-nine organs, there is apparently no universally standard of what constitutes an organ, according to Wikipedia. The most significant systems that are very important for humans to exist include the circulatory system, digestive system, endocrine system, immune system, lymphatic system, musculoskeletal system, nervous system, reproductive system, respiratory system, and urinary system. The most vital organs that are necessary for human survival are considered to be the brain, heart, kidneys, liver, and lungs. Every system in the body is incredibly orderly and intricate. While it is not the purpose of this writing to offer detailed information about all these systems and organs, it is important to point out certain parts of the human body. We will look at the brain, eyes, and the liver.

If we look at the human brain, we find an extremely complex organ. In his book *Creation: Remarkable Evidence of God's Design*, Grant Jeffrey describes the intricacy and complexity of the human brain:

> The hundred billion neurons in our brain are intricately linked to each other in the most intricate and complex network in the known Universe. Every one of these billions of neurons is connected to other neurons in a staggering number of complicated inter-connections. Every single neuron is directly connected with more than fifty thousand other neurons through the incredibly small fibers, called dendrites, allowing instantaneous transfers of messages across your brain. There are more than one quadrillion intricate electrical connections, or synapses, within the brain, making it the most phenomenally complex machinery scientists have discovered in the Universe.[2]

The more one studies the brain, the more one can see how incredible and how intricate it is. This description helps us to comprehend this fact more easily when we digest this information. It is not my intent to belabor the point.

A look at the human eye reveals a very complex and intricate optical system. Grant Jeffrey describes the complexity and sophistication of merely the retina of the eye:

To appreciate the complexity and sophistication of the design of the eye, we need to understand the function of the retina. The retina lines the back of the eye and acts as a type of film, receiving the actual image composed of light photons passing through the iris, cornea, and eye fluid. Your retina is thinner than paper, yet its tiny surface (only one-inch square) contains 137 million light-sensitive cells. Approximately 95 percent of these cells are rods that can analyze black-and-white images, while the balance of approximately seven million cone cells analyze color images. Each of these millions of cells is separately connected to the optic nerve, which transmits the signal to your brain at approximately three-hundred miles per hour. The millions of specialized cells in your eye can analyze more than one million messages a second and then transmit the data to the brain.[3]

A deeper and more in-depth study of the eye will reveal even more details about its remarkable abilities and functions. Suffice it to say that these aforementioned remarks demonstrate the complexity and ability of the eye. Can we truthfully claim the human eyes are the result of a series of accidents or random events?

The liver is the essential organ in a human body that purifies the blood that flows through the body. Grant Jeffrey describes the purpose of the liver as follows:

> The liver is involved in the essential production of glucose, which forms the main energy that allows our

body to function. Our body is constantly exposed to enormous amounts of chemical poisons and harmful waste substances that are naturally produced by our organs and cells in the normal course of our life. Our liver is found on the right side of the upper abdominal cavity and fulfills its essential function as the primary filter to remove the dangerous toxins from our blood's circulatory system. The role of the kidney is to work in tandem with the liver by removing a variety of water-soluble excess materials and poisons from our body.[4]

The brain, eye, and liver are simply three examples of many complex and intricate organs that perform vital functions for the human body. These organs appear to be very precisely designed and function precisely for their intended purpose. Whether one discusses the heart or other organs in a body, they are similarly intricate in design and function in accordance with their design. They have specific purposes and are very efficient as they are supposed to be. These examples are sufficient to raise doubts that they were created by accident or by random or by the laws of nature on their own.

Life Science noted a number of interesting facts about humans. The human body contains nearly 100 trillion cells. The average adult takes over 20,000 breaths a day. Each day the kidneys process about 200 quarts of blood to filter out about two quarts of waste and water. The human brain contains about 100 billion nerve cells. Finally, water makes up more than 50% of the average adult's body weight. These are remarkable facts, and it is quite important to note these facts as we continue our exploration of science. Thus, we can see that the human body is very complex and highly organized.

Astronomy

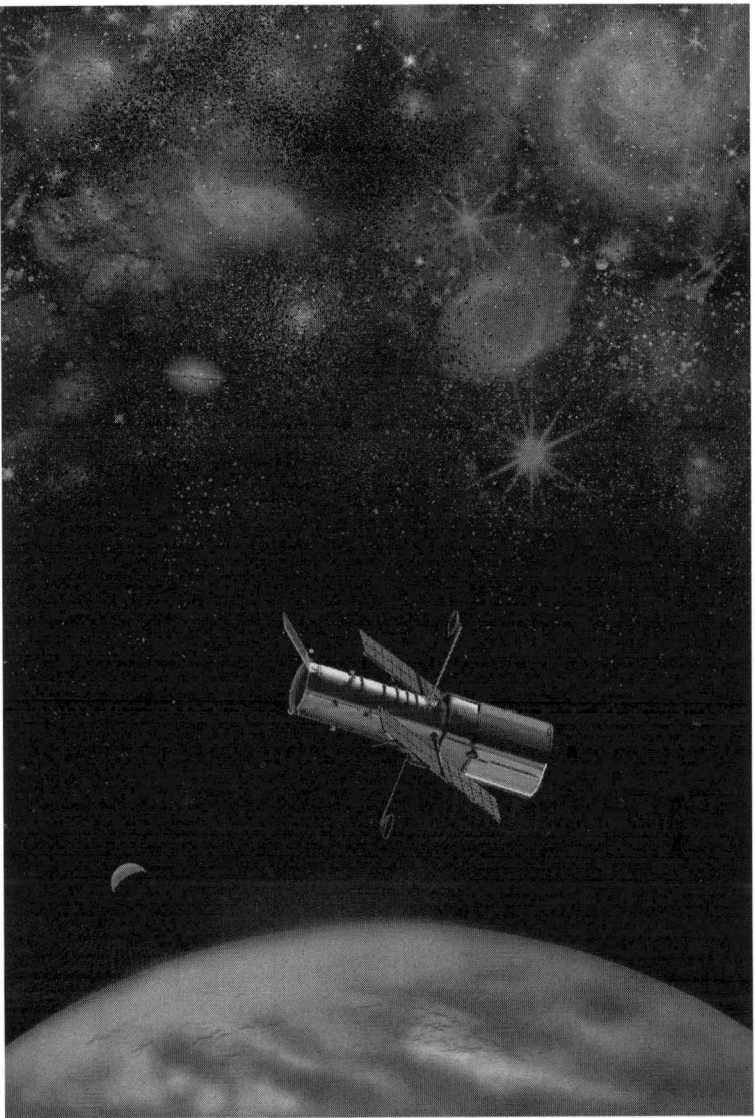

Now let us turn to astronomy. Typically, when we think of astronomy, most of us simply look up at the sky at night and admire all the stars in the sky. We don't know how many stars there are or how far away they are from our earth. Some people know something about the numerous constellations that we see, but most of us have little interest in knowing those things. A number of years ago, when I visited my older brother, a retired aeronautical engineer for NASA at Marshall Space Flight Center (MSFC) in Huntsville, Alabama, he took me to tour the Space and Rocket Center Museum located near MSFC. During our visit, one of the guides told me that there are billions of stars in our Milky Way galaxy and billions of galaxies in our universe. Recently, I read on the internet that there are reportedly 100 billion galaxies in our universe. If we try to calculate how many stars are in our galaxies and in our universe, we can figure for sure that there are a huge number of stars. When we really think about it, that concept staggers our imagination to say the least.

Are we to assume—without space travel and actual investigation of the universe—that we human beings are the only intelligent lifeforms in the entire universe? We might very well conclude that we are the only beings in our galaxy. That might seem reasonable at first glance, but can we assume scientifically that there are no other lifeforms in this or other galaxies? No, indeed, we cannot. Simple probability theory would dispel that notion. If we think about it, how can we assert that it is not possible that there are other lifeforms in a universe that is so huge? Again, Probability Theory suggests that there could be other lifeforms in our own galaxy and that there are most certainly other lifeforms in other galaxies throughout the entire universe. If so would it not make sense that there are some lifeforms more advanced than we are and some lifeforms less advanced than we are? It is easy to dismiss the notion of other lifeforms, but we will never learn the truth without investigating further. Without even going into space, on earth, we know some people in various countries are quite advanced in Europe, Asia, and South America, as examples, while there are some tribes who are less advanced in Africa, South America, and Australia, as other examples. It is important to note that these continents have both advanced and less advanced people. No continent is necessarily all one way or all the other. Since we have this kind of diversity among peoples on earth, doesn't it make sense that such diversity most likely exists among different planets in different galaxies, as we look at the whole universe?

It is no surprise to us to understand that we have a lot to learn about our universe, let alone our galaxy. A few years ago, when my wife and I visited Florence, Italy, we learned about Galileo, who shocked the Roman Catholic Church and the intellectuals of his day when he announced that contrary to the belief of most people, the earth revolved around the sun instead of the sun revolving around the earth. He shattered the ego-centric viewpoint that most people had in his day. It so shocked the Church that the Pope put him under house arrest and tried to destroy his credibility. The Pope would not tolerate such sacrilegious views and would not allow Galileo to corrupt the thinking of people in general. Interestingly, the scientific view that Galileo espoused outlasted the foolishness that the Pope erroneously supported. While many people know about Galileo, few people remember the name of the Pope who imprisoned the great man in his own house.

While we have highlighted three areas as examples, what do other disciplines tell us about science? The laws of physics and chemistry add to the complexity and orderliness in the world and the universe. Democritus conceived the concept that all things were made of a finite number of discrete particles. If we consider mathematics which includes geometry, does it support the previous point made about the organization and logic of the different disciplines of science? This leads us to take a deeper look into mathematics and some other sciences to give us a better perspective to answer our basic question.

CHAPTER 3

A Deeper Look at Human Knowledge

While we have previously highlighted three areas as examples, let's take a look at some other disciplines and see what we can learn. We will review mathematics, chemistry, and physics. Knowledge is composed of many different sciences and other disciplines, and we will learn quite a bit from this review of some of these other disciplines. A more exhaustive review of all the disciplines of science will not be needed to answer our basic question.

Mathematics

We begin with mathematics. According to the *American Heritage Student Dictionary*, mathematics can be defined as, "The study of the measurement, relationships, and properties of quantities and sets, using numbers and symbols. Arithmetic, algebra, geometry, and calculus are branches of mathematics."[5] Wikipedia quotes Galileo Galilei (1564-1642), "The universe cannot be read until we have learned the language and become familiar with the characters in which it is written. It is written in mathematical language, and the letters are triangles, circles, and other geometrical figures, without which means it is humanly impossible to comprehend a single word. Without these, one is wandering about in a dark labyrinth." Mathematics is utilized in many fields, including business, finance, natural science, engineering, medicine, and social sciences.

School children learn lessons in basic arithmetic that includes addition, subtraction, multiplication, and division. It is quite clear that school children complete these arithmetic calculations with specific steps to reach logical answers. Multiplication problems demonstrate a determined or calculated result. As an example, eight times four equals thirty-two. Other examples are: Six times eight equals forty-eight. Four times four equals sixteen. Many formulas are used by people to describe important relationships such as one in which "d" stands for distance, "r" stands for rate, and "t" stands for time. The basic formula is $d = r * t$, which means the distance equals the rate times time. If one wants to calculate the rate, one merely converts the formula mathematically to $r = d/t$. Other changes in the formula describe other relationships mathematically.

As aforementioned algebra is another branch of mathematics. According to Wikipedia, algebra is "the study of mathematical symbols and the rules for manipulating these symbols." Algebra is generally considered to be essential to study more deeply in mathematics, science, or engineering. It also has application in medicine and economics. It focuses on generalizations of arithmetic operations. Students use letters to stand for numbers; for example, they find solutions to problems as simple as $x + 6 = 8$ or more complicated problems such as $ax^2 + bx + c = 0$. The latter is known as a quadratic equation. In other words, algebra allows us to have an unknown quantity in an equation and to solve that equation to determine the value of that unknown. Algebra can become very complex in numerous applications. However, as human knowledge has grown, algebra has grown in complexity as well. Nevertheless, there are organized rules and procedures when using algebra.

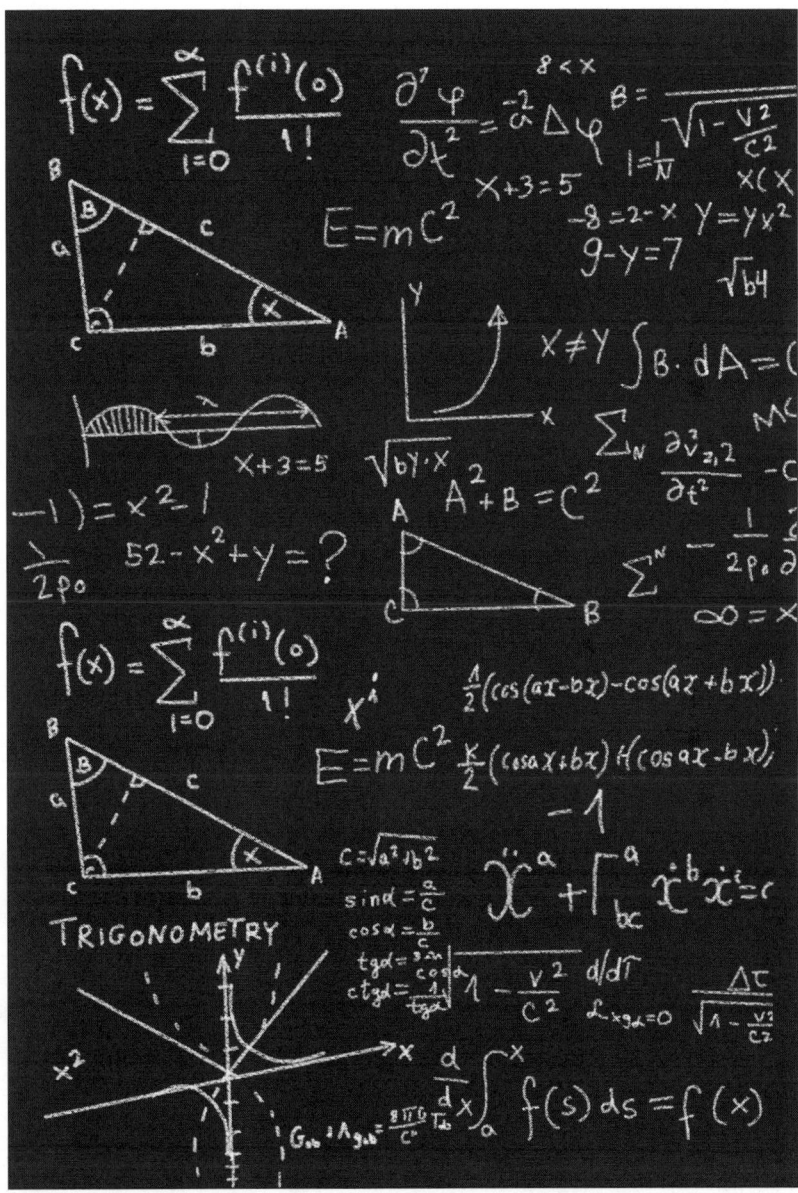

Geometry is another branch of mathematics that deals with the study of shape through studying angle properties, postulates, and theorems. A postulate is a proposition that has not been proven to be true, but it is considered to be true for the purpose of mathematical reasoning. Theorems are statements that have been proven to be true. Another concept that is used in geometry is the idea that angles are congruent if they are measured in degrees and are equal. Congruent angles do not have to point in the same direction.

Calculus, another branch of mathematics, has two main areas of application. They are differential calculus which focuses on rates of change and slopes of curves and integral calculus which focuses on the accumulation of quantities and the areas under and between curves. Isaac Newton and Gottfried Wilhelm Leibniz are generally credited with developing modern calculus in the 17th century. Today calculus is used in science, engineering, business, and economics. Studying calculus is a basic step to learning more advanced courses in mathematics. So, it, too, becomes more sophisticated and complex as one advances in their mathematical studies.

Chemistry

The next science we need to examine is chemistry. Chemistry studies properties, structures, and reactions of matter focusing on the atomic scale. In other words, Wikipedia defines chemistry as, "the scientific discipline involved with compounds composed of atoms, *i.e.* elements and molecules *i.e.* combinations of atoms: their composition, structure, properties, behavior and the changes they undergo during a reaction with other compounds." Traditional chemistry studies elementary particles, atoms, molecules, substances, metals, and other categories of matter. This matter can be in the form of solid, liquid, or gas states. The atom is a basic unit of chemistry. Its core is made up of positively charged protons, uncharged neutrons, and negatively charged electrons. A chemical element is a pure type of atom that has a particular number of protons in the nuclei that is known as the atomic number and is represented as a particular symbol. The standard way to show the chemical elements is in the Periodic Table that shows the elements by atomic number. The Periodic Table is arranged in groups, columns, and rows. It is not the purpose of this writing to analyze or discuss the Periodic Table, which is quite useful and remarkable for scientists and students alike.

PERIODIC TABLE

	1	2	3	4	5	6	7	8	9	10	11	12	13	14	15	16	17	18
1	1 H																	2 He
2	3 Li	4 Be											5 B	6 C	7 N	8 O	9 F	10 Ne
3	11 Na	12 Mg											13 Al	14 Si	15 P	16 S	17 Cl	18 Ar
4	19 K	20 Ca	21 Sc	22 Ti	23 V	24 Cr	25 Mn	26 Fe	27 Co	28 Ni	29 Cu	30 Zn	31 Ga	32 Ge	33 As	34 Se	35 Br	36 Kr
5	37 Rb	38 Sr	39 Y	40 Zr	41 Nb	42 Mo	43 Tc	44 Ru	45 Rh	46 Pd	47 Ag	48 Cd	49 In	50 Sn	51 Sb	52 Te	53 I	54 Xe
6	55 Cs	56 Ba	57 La	72 Hf	73 Ta	74 W	75 Re	76 Os	77 Ir	78 Pt	79 Au	80 Hg	81 Tl	82 Pb	83 Bi	84 Po	85 At	86 Rn
7	87 Fr	88 Ra	89 Ac	104 Rf	105 Db	106 Sg	107 Bh	108 Hs	109 Mt	110 Ds	111 Rg	112 Cn	113 Nh	114 Fl	115 Mc	116 Lv	117 Ts	118 Og

58 Ce	59 Pr	60 Nd	61 Pm	62 Sm	63 Eu	64 Gd	65 Tb	66 Dy	67 Ho	68 Er	69 Tm	70 Yb	71 Lu
90 Th	91 Pa	92 U	93 Np	94 Pu	95 Am	96 Cm	97 Bk	98 Cf	99 Es	100 Fm	101 Md	102 No	103 Lr

One can break down chemistry into three principal areas that students usually study. These are physical chemistry, organic chemistry, and inorganic chemistry. Physical chemistry is the study of the physical and fundamental aspects of chemical systems and processes. Sub-branches of this area include chemical kinetics, electrochemistry, quantum chemistry, solid-state chemistry, spectroscopy, and thermochemistry. Organic chemistry is the study of structure, properties, composition, and reactions of organic compounds. When a compound has carbon in it, it is normally an organic compound. Sub-branches include bio-chemistry, bioorganic chemistry, medicinal chemistry, physical organic chemistry, and polymer chemistry. Finally, inorganic chemistry is the study of properties and reactions of inorganic compounds or compounds that lack carbon. There are numerous other areas of chemistry that are utilized by professional chemists and scientists. All these categories demonstrate how vast, complex, and organized this subject really is. Chemistry is now sub-dividing atoms into even smaller particles, however, it is not the purpose of this study to delve into these deeper concepts. The basic point is that chemistry is an organized, complicated field of study.

Physics

Now we turn to the subject of physics. According to Wikipedia, physics is defined as "the natural science that studies matter and its motion and behavior through space and time and that studies the related entities of energy and force." As one of the most fundamental branches of science, its main purpose is to understand how the universe behaves. In the 16th and 17th centuries, Europeans used experimental and quantitative methods to discover what are now known as laws of physics. Discoveries found that the earth revolved around the sun instead of the sun revolving around the earth. Nicholas Copernicus was a leader in that effort. Johannes Kepler determined the laws that governed the motion of planetary bodies. Galileo Galilei did pioneering work on telescopes and observational astronomy. Isaac Newton discovered laws of motion and universal gravity. During the Industrial Revolution, more discoveries in thermodynamics, chemistry, and electromagnetics uncovered more scientific laws. Max Planck did important work to reveal quantum theory while Albert Einstein developed his famous theory of relativity. The progress of science goes on and on beyond these beginnings. Physics includes classical mechanics, acoustics, optics, thermodynamics, and electromagnetism.

Classical mechanics focuses on nature as continuous. In contrast, quantum theory focuses on the discrete nature of many phenomena at the atomic and subatomic level and with the aspects of particles and waves in describing such phenomena. The theory of relativity describes phenomena that take place in which an object is in motion with respect to an observer. Both quantum theory and the theory of relativity have applications in all areas of physics. Although these two theories are not scientific laws because they have not yet been proven to be fact, they are very widely believed to be true in the scientific community.

We can see how vast, organized, and complex physics really is as we already discussed about chemistry. This is so true of the many branches of science. While a particular branch may not be quite as organized with numerous levels as botany, they all are extensive, meaningful, and complicated. Next, let us turn to a more focused look at the Scientific Method and the laws of science.

CHAPTER 4

Scientific Method and Laws of Science

A scientific law is a concise statement of a relation that expresses a fundamental principle such as Newton's law of gravity. What eventually becomes a scientific law starts out as a theory or a basic idea or proposal typically based on a set of observations made by a scientist. The process that follows to prove its validity is called the Scientific Method.

In his well-known book, *A Brief History of Time*, Stephen Hawking describes two criteria that a theory must satisfy to be a "good theory" or a scientific law. Hawking says, "It must accurately describe a large class of observations on the basis of a model that contains only a few arbitrary elements, and it must make definite predictions about the results of future observations."[6] In other words, a scientist observes certain things happening and postulates that those things will continue to happen if those criteria occur again. Hawking cites that Aristotle believed Empedocles' theory that everything was made out of four elements which were earth, air, fire, and water. While the idea was simple, Hawking points out that it failed to offer any "definite" predictions. In contrast

Newton proposed his theory of gravity in a simpler model, but it predicts the motions of the sun, the moon, and the planets "to a high degree of accuracy." Hawking goes on to say, "...You can *disprove* a theory by finding even a *single* observation that disagrees with the predictions of the theory [Emphasis mine]."[7] As long as new experiments repeatedly agree with the predictions, the theory "survives," but whenever a new observation is found to disagree, "we have to abandon or modify the theory," says Hawking.[8]

Hawking proclaims, "The whole history of science has been the gradual realization that events do not happen in an arbitrary manner but that they reflect a certain underlying order..."[9] Over time humankind has learned so much about the various areas of science including in chemistry and physics. When we look at chemistry, we find numerous laws that have been discovered over a long time. Following are some of the more commonly-known laws as examples.

Avogadro's Law says, "Equal volumes of different gases under identical temperatures and pressure conditions will contain equal numbers of molecules." Boyle's Law says, "At constant temperature, the volume of a confined gas is inversely proportional to the pressure to which it is subjected."

Charles' Law says, "At constant pressure, the volume of a confined gas is directly proportional to the absolute temperature."

Dalton's Law says, "The pressure of a mixture of gases is equal to the sum of the partial pressures of the component gases."

Faraday's Law says, "The weight of any element liberated during electrolysis is proportional to the quantity of electricity passing through the cell and also to the equivalent weight of the element."

The First Law of Thermodynamics says, "The total energy of the universe is constant and is neither created nor destroyed."

In classical physics and in atomic physics, we find many commonly-known laws as well. Examples are as follows: Ampere's Law says, "The line integral of magnetic flux over a closed surface is directly proportional to the algebraic sum of the current flowing through the surface."

Coulomb's Law says, "The attractive or repulsive force between two charges is directly proportional to the product of the charges and inversely proportional to the square of the distance between them."

One of Newton's laws of motion states, "A body at rest or in motion continues at rest or in motion unless an outside force acts upon it."

Ohm's Law says, "The potential difference between any two points in a circuit equals the current times the resistance."

Einstein's mass-energy equation says, "The energy of a particle is equal to the product of mass and square of the velocity of light." Many people are familiar with his famous equation $E = mc^2$.

Gauss' Law tells us, "The electric flux over a closed surface is directly proportional to the sum of the charges within the surface."

Newton's Law of Universal Gravitation says, "The force of attraction between two bodies is directly proportional to the product of the masses of the bodies and inversely proportional to the square of the distance between them."

It is not the purpose of this writing to discuss these laws or how these laws are applied. The point I make is that these and other laws exist and must be reckoned with by scientists in their studies, observations, experiments, and judgments notwithstanding the fact that it took humankind many years to discover these laws. These laws govern our efforts to study and learn more about all areas of science.

Despite being an avowed atheist, Paul Davies stated his belief, "that the laws of nature [*i.e.* science] are real objective truths about the universe and that we discover them rather than invent them."[10] Davies further points out that these laws exist independently of other knowledge. There are "regularities," patterns, and rhythms that are found in life even extending to atoms and "their constituents." Davies states unequivocally, "The existence of regularities in nature [*i.e.* science] is an objective mathematical fact."[11]

Classical physics offers a set of fundamental theories, which describes the nature of ordinary or macroscopic scale. However, scientists made observations which could not be reconciled with classical physics. Max Planck "solved" a black-body radiation problem, during which time he developed his quantum theory which may also be referred to as quantum mechanics. Quantum mechanics normally applies to atoms, molecules, and subatomic particles, but Planck and his followers now also apply his theory to the universe. Planck won the Nobel Prize for physics in 1918 for his theory.

Another change from classical physics is Heisenberg's Uncertainty principle, "which states that all measurable quantities (e.g. position, momentum, energy) are subject to unpredictable fluctuations in their values."[12] If scientists follow the scientific method to examine evidence about the existence of God, they will begin to answer the basic issue. The more they examine the evidence and the laws of science, the more they will understand about the existence of God. They cannot ignore the scientific method to reach a truthful conclusion. And they cannot distort the scientific method or make assumptions to claim truth for their prejudices or incompetent studies. Part of their study and examination must include how the laws of science were created. The laws themselves had no power or ability to create themselves, and they supposedly did not exist until they were discovered. If scientists can prove by empirical evidence that they existed before the universe was created, let them offer that proof. It is foolish to offer statements that we cannot prove.

Next, we will turn to studying the Big Bang Theory and the main theories about the origin of life as we continue our exploration to answer the basic question about whether or not God exists.

CHAPTER 5

The Big Bang Theory and Origin of Life Reviewed

Both Stephen Hawking and Paul Davies describe numerous theories expounded by many scientists. While Hawkins seems to focus more on mainstream conjectures, Davies offers a more comprehensive presentation of various theses. In fact, Davies describes strengths and weaknesses of numerous theories. In this chapter, I will discuss a third theory of creation offered by Sjoerd L. Bonting. Then I will focus on Paul Davies' ideas about the creation of the universe, the beginning of life, life on Mars and how that affected the earth, and the issue of "progressive" evolution.

As Stephen Hawking, Paul Davies, and others suggest, most scientists seem to believe the universe began with the Big Bang. The Big Bang theory is a cosmological model that describes how the universe began as a very high-density and high-temperature state and subsequently expanded to the point where it is now. Apparent measurements of the expansion rate of the universe motivated scientists to estimate the occurrence of the Big Bang at roughly 13.8 billion years ago and thus gives us the approximate age of the universe. Supposedly, after the initial expansion, the universe cooled sufficiently to allow the formation of subatomic particles and then atoms. The stars and galaxies formed later. Scientists suggest that the expansion of the universe is accelerating in more recent times. They claim that the known physical laws of nature can be used to calculate aspects of the universe in detail back in time to the initial state of extreme density and temperature, or in other words, back to creation.

There is another well-known theory about how the universe began. It is called "creation out of nothing" or more officially as "*creatio ex nihilo.*" As Dr. Sjoerd L. Bonting, formerly Professor of Biochemistry at the University of Nijmegen, Holland and a priest in the Anglican Communion, noted the idea of creation out of nothing was introduced by Theophilus of Antioch around c. 185. Later, Augustine (c. 400) accepted *creatio ex nihilo,* which was almost universally accepted by the Church. It has not really been questioned by the Church since then.[13] Until now. According to this theory, God created the universe without pre-existing materials. There was no order; there was nothing in the beginning. The Bible describes the earth as a "formless void and darkness covered the face of the deep [Genesis 1:1-2]." The Bible has no further explanation of this statement.

Bonting states, "The Creator in Genesis is outside and above matter and the process of creation. He is absolute and timeless: in the words of Isaiah, 'I am the first and I am the last; besides me there is no god.'"[14]

Dr. Bonting proposes a third theory of creation, his own Chaos Theology. He maintains that God created the universe and the earth out of chaos by ordering it through three separations to negate chaos. The three separations were light from darkness, water from heaven, and earth from sea.[15] "My thesis and the centre of the chaos theology," says Bonting, "is that the remaining element of chaos in the creation expresses itself in the evil in the world, both physical (natural disasters and disease) and moral (human evil)."[16] He summarizes his theory by stating three essential points. First, God made the initial creation from an "unexplained initial chaos." Secondly, God battled creation in a continuing battle with "the remaining element of chaos." And thirdly, evil developed from "the remaining element of chaos."[17] He believes that his Chaos Theory helps to explain how the story of creation and science reconcile better together to increase a deeper understanding of the reality of creation. I saw and heard Bonting speak about 2005 at Holy Cross Episcopal Church in Castro Valley, California while I was searching for a new church. The most significant point that I learned from him at the time was that creation was still an on-going process and is not yet finished after the original six days of creation that we hear about. Scientists point out all the time how suns in the universe die out and disappear. Earthquakes and volcanic eruptions were merely two ways the earth changed and was transformed in various ways. These things give some credence to Bonting's claim, as I see it. I will not discuss Bonting's theory about the origin of evil. That is outside the purpose of this book and is left for another book or presentation.

To explain the beginnings of life, Paul Davies described three principle theories. Before presenting the three theories, Paul exclaims, "To be sure, we have a good idea of the where and the when of life's origin, but we are a very long way from comprehending the how."[18] The first theory to explain the beginning of life is the chemical self-assembly in a watery medium somewhere on the earth. Secondly, he mentions viable microbes traveled to earth from space and in particular from Mars. Thirdly, the idea suggests that life began deeply inside the earth.[19] Most of the development of life occurred in the last billion years, says Paul. It is not the purpose of this writing to delve further to explain these theories. For further information, the reader is referred to the Paul Davies' book that is cited.

Davies begins his discussion about the origin of life by defining "life." He says there are nine physical properties of life. These include the following: Autonomy, Reproduction, Metabolism, Complexity, Organization—organized complexity, growth and development, information content, hardware and software entanglement, permanence and change.[20] Again, it is not the purpose of this writing to delve further to explain these physical properties. For further information, the reader is referred to the Paul Davies' book that is cited. Davies points out that each of us has a secret code within us. This code is called DNA and contains instructions on how to make a human being. According to Davies, this DNA code came into existence "spontaneously" created by Mother Nature. However, Davies admits, "Nobody knows how or where the first DNA molecule formed."[21] In other words, Davies cannot provide evidence of the creation of DNA or its source. It is basically his assumption, so he can avoid any explanation of its source.

In 1837, Charles Darwin reviewed his own thoughts and made a simple sketch to illustrate his concept about the theory that he was forming in his mind. The drawing was of an "irregularly branched" tree to show the history of plants and animals. This was his "tree of life." This sketch became a powerful tool to communicate his idea, which grabbed the imagination of many followers of his theory. This idea continued to dominate the thinking of many scientists for many years.

In line with Darwin's thinking, Davies offers several strong reasons to justify the idea that there is a universal ancestor or microbe for all human, animal, and plant life. He goes through all kinds of scientific explanations and gyrations to justify that conclusion. For example, Davies discusses how scientists divided all life into two domains until a subsequent scientist developed his argument that there are three domains. Then Davies admits there is the "still-unresolved question of how the three domains are situated on the tree of life."[22] But the thinking of many scientists breaks down when they discuss the first microbe and fail to prove how it was created and by whom.

Darwin's
Tree of Life

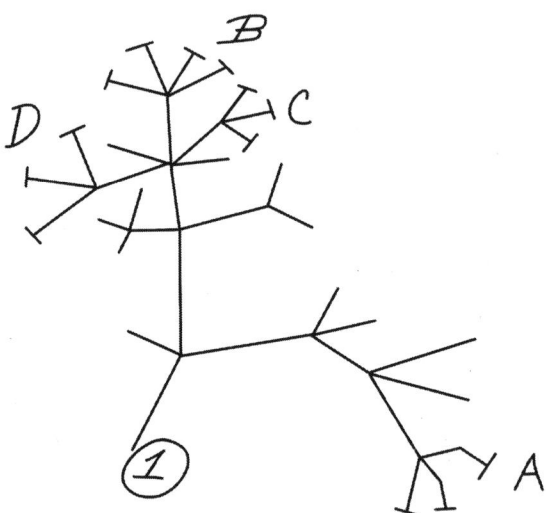

In 1862, Louis Pasteur performed a series of experiments to demonstrate that living organisms come only from other living organisms. In this way, Pasteur directly contradicted Charles Darwin's theory of evolution. According to Davies, the flaw in Darwin's theory was that he failed to explain how the *first* living organism was created. Then Davies postulated that, "Yet, in the absence of a miracle, life could have originated *only* by some sort of spontaneous generation [emphasis in the original]."[23] Davies offers his explanation of how these problems were overcome by scientists, but he again runs into the same basic problem that scientists fail to explain the source of the first atoms, first molecules, first cell, or first microbe in the first place. They cannot seem to explain the origin of those "firsts."

Repeatedly, Davies makes comments, such as "Life is not haphazard complexity, it is organized."[24] Davies admits that some "science" is not really actual experiments to find the truth, "So far most of the 'experiments' have been computer simulations rather than the real thing [i.e. actual experiments]."[25] Computer simulations have significant limitations. If the simulation is not comprehensive enough, it can lead to inaccurate, if not, wrong, conclusions. It is wise to remember any little flaw in the computer program can produce false results. The old saying about computers remains valid: "Garbage in, garbage out." How do scientists know absolutely that those computer programs do not contain flaws in the program? Davies adds to his observation about life, "Life is in fact *specified*—*i.e.* genetically directed—organization."[26] DNA instructs the characteristics of living things.

In a summary, Davies proclaims, "The record of the genes suggests that the universal ancestor lived deep beneath the Earth's surface, at a temperature well above a hundred degrees Celsius, and probably ate sulfur."[27] And he adds, "We know almost nothing about the circumstances that connected the first living thing to the universal ancestor."[28]

One theory suggests that Mars had meteorites that traveled to earth to create life on earth. Microbes exist deeply inside of rocks on Mars. In this way, meteorites conveyed these microbes to earth. Davies tries to make the case that billions of years ago Mars had a lot of water, which affected the planet's surface. He asserts that Mars is "peppered" with craters and giant canyons and valleys where rivers "may" have flowed. However, he admits, "...No trace of water remains in Mars' ancient riverbeds; they have long dried up."[29] He further states that they dried up "at least" three and a half billion years ago. He concludes, "All this adds up to strong circumstantial evidence of hydrothermal systems on ancient Mars..."[30] Circumstantial evidence is normally NOT acceptable in a court of law, but why is it acceptable to "scientists?" It needs to be noted that in very recent days, NASA discovered water on Mars.

Another issue lies with the process of evolution. Davies tells us that in the classic conflict between evolution and the "Christian Church" at the present time clearly evolution is accepted by the overwhelming number of people. Then he raises the question about whether or not evolution is developing in a "progressive" manner. In other words, is evolution growing more and more in an upwards fashion as opposed to developing downwards? If life is gradually improving, in the 19th Century, it became common for learned people to believe that evolution was not a "meandering path" but rather a "ladder of progress." In other words, life grew directly upwards from microbes to humans. Davies asserts, "If evolution really is progressive, the laws of nature [i.e. science] might not only be rigged in favor of creating life, but rigged in favor of advancing it, too."[31]

In analyzing this notion of progressive evolution, Davies raises three objections. First, such a conclusion "implies a value judgment" in the sense that it suggests humans are better than "apes or frogs." Secondly, by sheer numbers, Davies asserts that the number of microbes outnumbers the number of humans on the earth. Thirdly, such a notion is "noxious" on ideological grounds.[32] Science is about scientific facts, not about values or about ideology. It appears Davies is trying to be politically correct with the common thinking of unscientific, biased people.

One might say that Davies cannot see the forest for the trees or his nose to spite his face on this issue. His first objection is negated by the fact that humans are more intelligent than apes, frogs, or microbes. That is not a value judgment; that is a scientific fact. Secondly, the fact that there are more microbes than humans is immaterial and does not compute, as they say. The first comment about greater human intelligence negates that second piece of nonsense. Thirdly, the third complaint is itself "noxious" and is without merit whatsoever. Period. It is utterly amazing that a so-called scientist is sidetracked by value judgments instead of scientific facts. Value judgments are not his or any scientist's specialty. They need to focus on what science proves instead of merely supporting their personal values or attitudes.

Another point to discuss is the "ladder of progress." How in the world does a scientist invent this concept? What grounds does one use to justify this analogy? There is nothing mentioned in science to merit this concept. It is quite reasonable to suggest that evolution is progressive. There is no real evidence to suggest that evolution has improved in so-called steps in a ladder as opposed to a process of gradual improvement over time. The latter point is actually the more accurate description of evolutionary process since creation. No one can legitimately argue that the process has been an even, steady process. There is no scientifically-proven reason why it could not have been steady at times and unsteady at times over the time since creation. Enough evidence has been provided that humans have developed over time as have other organisms. The fact that dinosaurs and other creatures on earth and in the sea have become extinct does not negate the process of evolution over the long term. My parents lived from 1902 until 1997. During that short period of time, humankind flew in the first successful airplane at Kitty Hawk and developed airplanes, radio, television, color television, automobiles, vaccines, cured illnesses, telescopes, satellites, computers, and landed on the moon to cite some progressive steps in the growth of humankind. When I was a teenager, I heard that humankind had learned more in the past ten years than in all human history combined and that humankind would learn more in the next ten years than all human history combined, INCLUDING the ten years just past. Since I took math in school up through calculus, I quickly understood the geometric progression that fact represented. One can see the growth of humankind in our own lifetimes. Wars and dictatorships and other events do not negate this progress.

Davies quotes Stephen Jay Gould, one of the scientists he discusses, "We are *glorious accidents* of an unpredictable process with no drive to complexity, not the expected results of evolutionary principles that yearn to produce a creature capable of understanding the mode of its own necessary construction [emphasis mine]."[33] Humankind has advanced in many ways from Neanderthal man to Cro-Magnon man to current humans. History records that humans have advanced from the Stone Age to the Bronze Age to the Iron Age to the present. Humankind has developed through various civilizations, including Babylon, Greece, Rome, the Mongols, Huns, and Turks. Humans are progressing in their ability to think and reason. Many years ago, I visited Timbuktu in Mali. Timbuktu, I learned, was a thriving trade center and center of knowledge while Europe was in the Dark Ages. In more recent history, humankind is developing more sophisticated cars, airplanes, computers, telephones, medical advancements, and other things. All of this demonstrates undeniable, directed progress—not simply accidents or growth by chance.

When some scientists claim that the development of life was a series of "glorious accidents," it is virtually impossible for the number of "glorious accidents" to occur to develop seven levels deep of organization that exist in botany and biology as discussed in a previous chapter. The number of accidents would have to be so large that such a theory makes no sense. Repeatedly, Davies mentions how organized life is, although he does not connect the dots that there is a force or intelligence that is behind such organization. Davies begins by stating his assumption that there is no God and refuses to permit himself to deviate from his stated assumption.

When scientists, like Paul Davies and Stephen Jay Gould, offer all kinds of speculation, conjectures, and gossip, how can they simply or legitimately as scientists deny God's existence? If they claim to be legitimate scientists, then they must also consider and examine scientific evidence to prove whether or not God exists. To simply assume or deny that God (as Paul Davies categorically states) does not exist is not real science. So, Davies and others prevent themselves from searching for, discovering, and evaluating evidence of a higher intelligence that could have created the universe, earth and all that is contained therein. Making assumptions precludes discovery in itself. Too many scientists are so focused on the minutiae of their specialty that they cannot see a broader picture. Too many scientists are so self-centered, egotistical, selfish, or foolish who do not think and who pedantically and falsely claim to be scientists. Reading Paul Davies book, *The 5th Miracle: The Search for the Origin and Meaning of Life*, shows that a lot of scientists make more phony claims that lack common sense than one would think was reasonable. They offer little evidence to solidly substantiate their wild claims. History is replete with scientific "facts" that have been proven to be false or incorrect over the centuries to say the least. Americans know very well the lesson that Christopher Columbus taught his generation and future generations when he proved that the earth was not flat as people generally thought at that time. The lesson is that scientists need to find the evidence that supports and contradicts the issue of the existence of God. Then they need to evaluate that evidence objectively to reach a logical and accurate conclusion. In other words, they should be scientists instead of politicians or simple-minded fools who spout politically-correct nonsense.

Since we have reviewed and considered the Big Bang Theory and the scientific view of the origin of life, it is appropriate to review and consider creation according to the Bible.

CHAPTER 6

Creation According to the Bible

It is only fair to review and consider the view of creation from the perspective of the Bible. So, let us discuss it.

The Bible says, "In the beginning when God created the heavens and the earth, the earth was a formless void and darkness covered the face of the deep, while a wind from God swept over the face of the waters. Then God said, 'Let there be light,' and there was light. And God saw that the light was good; and God separated the light from the darkness. God called the light Day, and the darkness he called Night. And there was evening and there was morning, the first day."[34]

And God said, 'Let there be a dome in the midst of the waters, and let it separate the waters from the waters.' So, God made the dome and separated the waters under the dome from the waters that were above the dome. And it was so. God called the dome Sky. And there was evening and there was morning, the second day."[35]

The Bible goes on to describe that God subsequently created land that He called Earth and the waters He called Seas. Next, He created vegetation, including plants and fruit trees. This was on the third day. On the fourth day, God created the sun and the moon. On the fifth day, God created sea creatures of all kinds as well as birds over the land. Then God created all kinds of animals, like cattle plus many kinds of insects and wild animals on the sixth day. Finally, God created human beings. On the seventh day, God rested.[36]

How did God create the universe, the earth, and human beings? Science and theologians frequently assert that the universe and the earth were created out of nothing, a concept called *"creatio ex nihilo."* Many physicists offer numerous theories how the earth came into being out of nothing. They offer all kinds of gyrations to substantiate their allegations. The physicists most commonly support the Big Bang theory in which a giant explosion created the universe and the earth. As Sjoerd Bonting and other physicists point out, even an explosion must have some materials and particles to have a real explosion. How can an explosion occur if there is nothing to explode? Isn't it clear that if nothing explodes, it yields nothing as a result? In contradiction to science, theologians claim God created everything out of nothing. Does God's existence depend on that claim being true? Some theologians appear to be afraid when some critics claim that God must be part of the creation; instead they say that God must transcend the creation.

If God is the creator of the universe, doesn't that imply that God is greater than the universe? The Bible provides an overview of creation rather than a step-by-step description of how God created everything. The Bible is very interesting in how it describes the general steps God took as He created everything. Science, on the other hand, attempts more precisely to describe the specific steps of creation. As time passes and as new scientists replace scientists of the past, they discover newer facts and become more and more informed how things happened. When they describe the Big Bang theory, they get close to the actual point of creation but cannot quite explain the actual point of creation. Subsequent generations will learn how to more and more accurately describe creation. Perhaps the Big Bang theory is correct, and perhaps it will be replaced by a more accurate theory as the process of thesis, antithesis, and synthesis continues throughout many more generations of physicists and other scientists. As history has clearly demonstrated so many times that it's beyond counting, what was true in the past gets corrected in the future. It is indisputable that scientific "facts" change over time.

How does a builder build a house? First, the builder typically develops a plan for what he wants to build. Then he gathers the materials for the building. Next, he builds the foundation of the house and later builds the walls and the rest of the building as he envisions it. Jesus talked about a builder building a solid foundation as he begins to build a house. Is it unreasonable or outlandish to think that before creation, God developed a plan how he wanted to create the universe, the galaxies, and the planets in the various galaxies, plus the sea creatures, the vegetation, cattle, insects, and wild animals, as well as human beings and everything else? The steps described in Genesis indicate clear, deliberate steps in the process of creation. For example, God created the land before He created the vegetation. In another example, God created animals like cattle before He created humans. In other words, He took steps in logical order. That seems pretty clear.

It is not unthinkable that He created the materials He needed to create what He planned to do first. The Bible does not say specifically that He spoke the universe or the earth into existence. It does say He spoke to create light. So, speaking was at least one tool and technique of how God created. The Bible does not purport to describe every detail of creation. Thus, God could have snapped His fingers to create or threw lighting into the space where He chose to create the universe or took action in numerous other ways He chose to create. He could have even used explosions as a means of creation. As the Supreme Being, God is not, and was not, limited to only one tool or only one technique during creation. It is quite reasonable and plausible for God to have utilized numerous means of creation.

The first sentence in the Bible says, "In the beginning, when God created the heavens and the earth, the earth was a formless void and darkness covered the face of the deep, while a wind from God swept over the face of the waters." This sentence does not state that God used his voice to speak the creation of the heavens and the earth. It states that "God created the heavens and the earth." Then it states, "…A wind from God swept over the face of the waters…" So, obviously the Bible states TWO ways that God created—His voice and a wind. So, in other words, God spoke things into existence, and He blew a wind. If God used two methods to create, why couldn't He have used three, four, five or more methods to create? Why do we humans set limits on God's power when we cannot prove those limits? How little is our faith to try to limit the Supreme Being to one method like we are HIS creators? It's just like we limit God in the creation story to creation in seven days from the perspective of humans instead of seven "days" from God's perspective. Theologians attempt to limit God into the little boxes they create for the Supreme Being. It is a joke to be so limited in one's thinking. And it's certainly unscientific as well!

Most people seem to agree that we humans ask some basic questions about our existence. Why are we here? Why does the universe exist? Is there a purpose to life in our universe? Is there a creator? Humans have asked these kinds of questions since humans first walked on the earth. To answer these questions, we have at least two fundamental schools of thought. One claims it was all created by God the Creator. Science-minded individuals suggest that the universe, the earth, and humans and all animal and plant life resulted due to random or accidental events through evolution during millions and millions of years. A key development that has allowed the "theory of evolution" to gain a significant upper hand and support in the debate among humans was Charles Darwin's book, *Origin of Species*, which claimed that all life developed through a materialistic, natural process. As a result, the account of creation described by the Bible lost adherents in big numbers.

Those people who believe in the Biblical account in Genesis believe many believers lose their faith when, in their opinion, science proves that the account in Genesis is simply a false myth. Those people believe that the opposing accounts cannot coexist. Either creation or the theory of evolution is correct. This is serious to some Christians because they put their faith in the Bible and trust it for their salvation and in the truthfulness of the teaching, life, death, and the supernatural resurrection of Jesus Christ, as the Bible says. They think that if evolution is true, then their faith in Christ is somehow weakened. They fear that they will be viewed as "double-minded," which means having two totally different and in fact contradictory beliefs at the same time. That makes some Christians weak in their faith.[37]

Jeffrey proclaims that the two theories directly contradict each other as he says, "This biblical doctrine of Creation…is in fundamental contradiction to the atheistic theory of evolution that denies the existence of God and claims that man lives in an accidental Universe without purpose, plan or design. If evolution is true, then the Bible and the words of Jesus Christ are false. It is as clear as that."[38] Not surprisingly, many scientists would proclaim the same thing. It is now clear why some Christians feel so threatened by science and the theory of evolution. This is so important to some Christians who feel the two theories are such opposites that there is no possibility that both theories can be true. If one is true, then the other theory must be false and vice versa. Some Christians believe they have a personal relationship with Jesus Christ based on what the Bible tells us including his "sacrifice on the Cross," His resurrection, and their hope for salvation, resurrection, and heaven. They tie together the creation story with the Biblical account of Jesus. If one is true, then the other is true. If one is false, then the other is false in their minds.

Other scientists and theologians believe that both theories can be true and neither theory negates the other. They believe they are not being "double-minded" at all. If we look at the Theory of Evolution by Charles Darwin, we remark that he wrote that theory in 1859[???]. The question arises whether or not the thinking and knowledge of humankind has advanced in any way since 1859 about his theory. Could the theory apply to some extent and not to some extent? How might we adjust his theory to be more accurate? Or is it possible to disprove his theory completely? Grant Jeffrey wrote his book, *CREATION: Remarkable Evidence of God's Design,* for the purpose to actually and completely disprove Charles Darwin's theory. He offers very credible evidence to make his case. It is not the purpose of this writing to prove or disprove Jeffrey's evidence and theory. It is left for the reader to make that determination for himself or herself. However, it raises enough evidence to question the validity of Darwin's theory.

There is another work that looks at how theology and physics interact with each other. So, we will take a look at that work.

CHAPTER 7

Physics and Theology

One very relevant work that needs to be examined is the book *God, Creation, and Contemporary Physics* by Mark William Worthing. He examines both physics and theology and looks at how each one offers valuable insights in these three subject areas listed in his book title and the exchange of dialogue between the two areas of God and physics. Worthing starts by admitting "two key assumptions." The first assumption "is that science can legitimately address questions related, at least indirectly, to the existence and role of God in our world."[39] His second assumption is that "while theology cannot critique the specifically scientific and technical aspects of physics, it is certainly free to analyze the relevance of the results of physics for theology as well as to critique the validity, consistency, and significance of those conclusions that are clearly metaphysical or theological in nature."[40] He goes on to favor a dialogue between theology that respects nature and a more humbled attitude by scientists instead of their usual know-it-all attitude.

Worthing discusses what he considers to be the three major arguments for God's existence, although he mentions five types of arguments. The three are ontological, cosmological, and teleological arguments. The ontological argument, he says, contends that God exists necessarily. The second cosmological argument originated with Aristotle and later expanded by Thomas Aquinas comes about because people have observed that everything in the world, including matter or movement, exists, even if it appears to exist by uncertainty or by chance is actually caused to exist. This cause is God. The third teleological argument is based on the natural, observable world. This argument, Worthing observes, is the fifth way that Thomas Aquinas claims proves the existence of God. To explain this argument more clearly, Worthing cites eighteenth-century theologian William Paley in his 1802 work, *Natural Theology*, who poses the concept that there is "so much beauty, order, harmony, and precision in the natural world that it must have been designed by a higher being who continues to govern the world."[41]

Worthing addresses the question about whether or not God could create out of nothing or in other words, *creatio ex nihilo*. "Natural science deals with matter, physical laws, and the relationships that exist between and within the physical realities of the universe. *But most of all, natural science deals with explanations* [Emphasis mine]."[42] The statement that natural science "deals with explanations" indicates that science cannot deal with a situation without an apparent explanation. In other words, one could say that if they cannot explain it, it cannot exist. It also demonstrates that science is a discipline in which the existence of anything must be physical and have a cause. This entire quote means that science cannot comprehend any notion that a superior being can create something out of nothing. So, science dismisses *creatio ex nihilo* as a concept of theology instead one of science.

Worthing tries to question the existence of God in terms of space and time. He poses the question, "How free could a Creator have been in choosing the initial conditions of the universe?"[43] If God is the Creator, He must have had total freedom to create creation as it happened, when it happened, and how it happened. The fact that He had millions of options to choose from does not obviate His ability and power to make the choices He made and caused. If He had the power to create such a huge universe, then He had the power to sort through so many basic options and to select the ones He desired for earth and for every other planet in every solar system in the universe. And He was not necessarily compelled to choose the identical options for earth that He chose for life forms on other planets in other solar systems. He could have chosen different conditions for life on planets in various solar systems. For example, He could have chosen a different mixture of gases on other planets instead of an oxygen rich environment that humans need in order to exist. Since humans have not yet visited other planets, let alone different solar systems, how can we dispute whether or not this supposition may be true or even false? If people have no ability to question God, it is equally true that it is foolish for even Einstein to question the extent of freedom that God had to do whatever He wanted during creation. If God is the Creator, He could do whatever He wanted to do, even if foolish scientists pedantically pretend that He couldn't. It is ridiculous for scientists to pretend that God must obey the limits that some scientists try to impose in their ignorance or shortsightedness after the fact and without direct observation or means to prove their allegation. If that were allowed, then anybody could make up an absurd story about God and merely claim it to be true just like some scientists do. Of course, the men of knowledge did, in fact, make up the absurd theory that the earth was flat. So, we have experience of learned men falsifying facts to fit their ignorance and prejudice. If God is the Creator, then He had—and has—the power to create whatever He wanted from nothing. He was—and is—greater than the universe instead of merely being a part of it.

Another concept that Worthing discusses is quantum physics. He points out, "Unlike classical physics, the fundamental assumption of quantum physics is indeterminism."[44] As Worthing noted, Werner Heisenberg formulated the uncertainty principle, which undermines the thinking that everything has a cause, although it supposedly does not strictly abandon causality or determinism. However, since there are many possible solutions, it obliges scientists to calculate possible outcomes on the basis of statistical probability. Worthing goes on to state that it is questionable as to how or even whether the uncertainty principle can be applied to large-scale "structures" in the universe. This raises the argument among scientists whether God is a mere spectator or a strict controller of events. Worthing notes that the determinism-indeterminism issue is a major dispute between classical and quantum physics.[45] Worthing moves on to discuss "singularities," which are unique, "non-repeatable" events that break down our ability to make predictions based on the laws of nature. He endeavors to relate singularities to miracles by God and the concept of evil, two subjects which are beyond the intent and scope of this work. So, we will leave those issues to another work.

Now, let us present a new theory about the existence of God and the origin of life.

CHAPTER 8

A New Theory Presented

The aim of this exploration and examination is to determine whether or not God exists. Let us now turn to answering the question. Can we verify or prove God exists? The reader may be surprised at how much proof exists to answer that question. So, let's present a new theory to explain and answer the question now.

First, it is necessary to point out that all human, animal, and plant life must be either directed or non-directed. There can be no other alternatives. Life cannot be half-directed and half non-directed or a quarter-directed and three-quarters non-directed or any other proportion that we might identify. If life is half-directed or some other proportion, we have to identify and account for WHO directs that half or portion. If some lifeform or superior being directs half or part of life, then it opens the discussion to explain why the lifeform doesn't direct all life. Thus, life is all one way or all the other—in other words, all directed or all non-directed.

If human, animal, and plant life is non-directed, then there can be no limitations on what kind of growth can develop. For example, humans can be born with three arms or four legs or fewer arms or legs or some other deviant physical differences. Or they can grow extra eyes, arms, legs, or other anomalies over a lifetime. As another example, animals can similarly be born with three legs instead of four legs or two heads instead of just one head, as well or any other deviation from the norm. Like humans, animals can develop mutations and changes in their bodies over a life span. As a third example, if you plant a certain plant, for example, corn, you could harvest potatoes instead or some other variant of corn or other plants. There would be no limitation on what plant life is produced or on how it is changed. Humans, animals, and plant life would be able to deviate in numerous ways at birth or over time. In short there would be no law of science that requires any order of life. DNA would be nonexistent.

However, as it is now, humans are typically born with one head, two arms, and two legs—consistently. That consistency means the birth and growth of a baby is limited or constricted in accordance to certain guidelines. Generally speaking those guidelines are strictly adhered to. Granted there are some babies born with deformities or abnormalities. However, those babies are exceptions to the general guidelines to which most babies adhere. Likewise animals follow similar guidelines. Plants also follow strict guidelines. If you plant corn, you will typically harvest the type of corn that was planted—no other variants or no other vegetable. That kind of limitation in human, animals, and plant life means that such life is directed. Such consistency in life is limited along specific guidelines, or as I suggest, directed.

When we looked at plant life, we found many levels of organization. They include kingdom, phylum, class, order, family, genus, and species.

If life is not directed, then every part of human, animal, and plant life *must* vary in innumerable directions and amounts. There can be no limits, such as evidenced by the many levels of organization. Anything can happen—because no limits exist. If all life is non-directed, then all life growth *must* deviate by accident or at random. One accident occurs after another. Or one random event occurs after another after another without any time limit. This means that human, animal, and plant life develops by accident or randomly without rhyme or reason and at any level of organization. The levels of organization listed above cannot exist if there is no directing force.

In contrast, if life is directed, then such extreme amount of organization is rational and clearly demonstrates an order caused by a directing force or intelligent life form that we may logically call God. We already noted that animal life is organized by the same categories or levels of organization. We also noted how organized the human body is. One might dismiss this notion by asserting that DNA requires such consistency in all life forms. However, this assertion fails to explain the cause for the existence of DNA. What is the cause of the DNA? That must be answered. Here it is suggested that God created DNA and all those levels of organization.

Science is built on the concept of cause and effect. In science we know there is a cause for everything. Are we going to claim that science demonstrates there is a cause for everything, except for the creation of our solar system—or our universe? *If there is a cause for everything, then there must be a cause for everything, including the galaxy and the universe.* There can be no exceptions. We cannot pick and choose where truth exists and deny it in other areas that may be inconvenient for us to believe. We discussed how huge our galaxy and our universe are. Can we presume to assert that such a vast array of billions of stars simply organized themselves in an arbitrary way or by accident into galaxies and developed the entire universe? If all life is non-directed, then we need to explain how all the orderliness can exist. If all life is directed, then an intelligent force created humans, all the laws of science, galaxies, and the entire universe. That intelligent force developed all things that were created in appropriate ways.

Despite being an avowed atheist, Paul Davies stated his belief "that the laws of nature [*i.e.* science] are real objective truths about the universe, and that we discover them rather than invent them."[46] Davies further points out that these laws exist independently of other knowledge. There are "regularities," patterns, and rhythms that are found in life, even extending to atoms and "their constituents." Davies states unequivocally, "The existence of regularities in nature [i.e. science] is an objective mathematical fact."[47]

We have to be honest and admit how little we know about other stars and galaxies. If we allow that intelligent life forms exist in galaxies outside our own solar system, we must acknowledge that there are life forms that may be more advanced than we are and some life forms that may be less advanced than we are. If we reach that conclusion, it is a small matter to admit that God may be a life form greater than we are and even greater in size and power than the entire universe. If we concede that, then it is a small step to admit that God may be a life form that is much greater than we are with huge powers. It is easy to see that God must be greater than the universe to be capable of creating the entire universe. That power is beyond human comprehension. If God is so huge or greater in size and power than the universe, then in contrast to God, a human must be smaller than a pebble of sand on the beach in comparison in terms of significance and power.

According to this theory, God created the universe and all the galaxies during a certain period of time. Scientists have estimated that occurred about "10,000 million years" ago. Because He is omnipotent, there was no limitation to His creative power at the time of creation. He did not need pre-existing matter, but He may have chosen to use pre-existing matter. He did not have any pre-existing physical laws or laws of the universe when he acted. However, that does not preclude that God may have chosen to create the laws of science to facilitate his acts of Creation. When scientists describe the creation in terms of the Big Bang, that theory may or may not be a true description of how God actually acted to accomplish the creation. So, whether He created in one way or another does not really matter. Science may in fact describe how God created the universe and the earth. That belief does not negate the fact that God was the Creator. After the creation of the universe, He created the earth, the seas, the mountains, the dry land, as well as the creatures of the sea and land and finally humans. He created the physical laws, or what we call the laws of the universe, that was part of the act of creation, no matter the sequence of His steps to accomplish His results. Laws cannot create themselves. There must be a source, a creator.

How can we interpret and explain the differences between the Bible and science? Who created the Bible? Who created science? While a young teenager, the author thought carefully and realized that God created the Bible by inspiring humans to write it, and He also created science. So, the author concluded that the Bible and science say the same thing. God cannot contradict Himself. So, the two must say the same thing, even though there are different languages and descriptions. The real difference between the Bible and science is basically humankind's misinterpretation of the Bible, misinterpretation of science and/or misinterpretation of both. As a young man, the author noticed that people used to quote the Bible, which claimed that 1,000 years is merely a blink of an eye to God. Nowadays more recent translations of the Bible phrase the same point somewhat differently, but they carry a similar meaning. The point is God, the Creator of the universe, cannot be confined to our human thinking process or sense of time, such as twenty-four hours in a day. If the Bible says that God created the whole world in six days and then rested, that does NOT mean God acted in accordance with humankind's perception of six twenty-four hour periods of time. It means that God acted in accordance with six days from God's perspective and outlook. In contrast science says that the creation and development of the earth and then humankind took millions and millions of years. If God is as immense a being as is suggested here, one day to God is most likely millions of years in the human perspective. Does it make sense to confine God to human limitations and perspectives? If we look at time in God's perspective, we probably will find six distinct periods of time while God performed his creation—in the manner described by the Bible—six God-days instead of six human days. And the seventh period, He rested.

Christians, and fundamentalist Christians in particular, should not be afraid to admit that and to recognize that God is so big and so powerful. They need to realize that He is greater in power and scope than the entire universe. Christians should glorify, honor, and praise God for being such a great, loving God. All people, and Christians in particular, need to understand that prejudice works for and against one's belief or disbelief in God. By having real faith in God, Christians especially need to understand that because He is so big and powerful, everything needs to be viewed and evaluated from *His* point of view and perspective instead of from a human's perspective. Then, things will become more clear and understandable. It is God who designed and created the universe, the planets, humankind, and everything else. It was not by accident or by random events over time, and it certainly was not created by any human. So, why would we view things from a human perspective? We do so only because we are so thoughtless and self-centered. Jesus advised us to seek the truth because it will set us free. We need to remember that.

Some so-called scientists argue that the discipline of science is limited to physical or naturalistic explanations. True science is open to ALL hypotheses, even the existence of a superior being or God. This theory focuses on physical and natural events and processes. This is not a religious treatise and does not advocate a theistic hypothesis based on the Bible or other religious writings. It advocates an evaluation of scientific evidence and use of deductive reasoning from the scientific evidence.

In summary, the theory presented is that all life including human, animal, and plant life is either directed or non-directed in its creation, growth and death. If all life is non-directed, its creation and growth must be by accident or at random, which permits existence and growth in all different directions and ways. If all life is directed, then a higher intelligent being causes life and growth on a consistent basis. Science is highly organized such as the levels of organization and thus provides in itself scientific evidence of the existence of God. Since the universe is so huge and beyond the comprehension of humankind, the Creator must be greater in size, scope, and power than humans.

CHAPTER 9

Related Ideas Examined

We will now turn to consider some issues that humankind raises to question the actions of God or to deny His existence. It is not our purpose to provide definitive answers to these issues but to provoke some real thought and discussion about the issues. However, these are the kinds of issues some critics bring up to deny the existence of God. So, we will examine and evaluate some of them in regard to that purpose. We will examine three issues in particular, which include major calamities in history, some basic interpretations of creation and science and inconsistencies in the Bible.

The first of the three issues to review are several of significant calamities that occurred over time. Let's discuss these events. After God created the Great Flood and advised Noah to build his ark, God promised to create a rainbow after every rain to remind Himself not to create another flood. God took action to prevent a repetition of another great flood. That avoided a stretch of time passing by before He acted. By creating and displaying a rainbow after it rains, He gave himself an immediate reminder that did not exist before God caused the Great Flood. This happened many years before God freed his people from the tyranny that His people suffered in Egypt.

A second calamity occurred when God allowed the Hebrews to be enslaved in Egypt for hundreds of years before He took action to "free his people." Is it because God didn't care what happened to the Hebrews? Or could it be possible that God had other issues or other intelligent beings to deal with in other parts of the universe? Could it be that God was distracted to other things than what was happening on the earth? Would it be possible that other events or matters had a higher priority that needed His attention more immediately? It would make sense to analyze and evaluate God's actions based on HIS point of view and HIS sense of time instead of humankind's point of view and sense of time. After all, how can the "created" judge the "Creator?" Over and over again, humankind makes this mistake. Repeating the same mistake over a long period of time—even centuries—does not solve the problem that humans face.

But centuries later, a third calamity occurred. The Nazi Holocaust. If God exists, why did He allow millions of people to be destroyed by the Nazi Holocaust? It is not the aim of this book to explain God's reasoning for His actions or lack of actions during the years the Nazis controlled Germany in the 20th century. The Bible reminds us that a human's wisdom is "foolishness in the sight of God." No human being can fully understand what God did or did not do or why He did or why He did not do anything. But since God probably looks at human events from the perspective of eternity—unlike a human's perspective of a few hours or perhaps days—God may have considered some factors that humans fail to account for. For example, God might not view human suffering for a relatively few years or death in horrible gas chambers as terrible from His long-range perspective as humans would think from their perspective because He might view the joy of going to heaven for eternity as more significant than short-term suffering that may quickly be forgotten. In other words, balancing all the years of eternity would weigh more heavily in God's perspective than a few years or brief moments of pain for humans. A woman suffers pain during child birth, but how much does she think about that pain in later years as the child grows up? Does she even remember it? She probably does not think much about that pain, generally speaking. So, it might be with God as He views people who suffer gas chambers, torture, or execution in various forms. During eternity those people might not remember that suffering as women don't think too much about their pain during pregnancy. Can any of us say for certain that this cannot be true? Does anyone know God's mind? The point is raised to offer a different perspective. Now let us turn to other issues.

The second of the three issues is how people interpret creation and science. Dr. Jason Lisle has a unique point of view that deserves examination. He summarizes his view of creation by describing worldviews first. He asserts, "First, everyone has presuppositions—basic beliefs that we take for granted before we begin to draw conclusions about the universe. These include things like laws of logic and the reliability of our senses. All of our presuppositions taken together form our *worldview*. Our worldview determines how we interpret the facts and even what constitutes a "fact." Dr. Lisle specifically points out, "Most people are not aware that they have a worldview, and consequently have not given much thought to it."[48] He asserts that one's worldview must be consistent and must follow certain rules, which we outline below.

We must follow three characteristics properly, according to Lisle. These are arbitrariness, inconsistency, and preconditions of intelligibility (AIP), and are listed and subdivided as follows. He uses these points to criticize the arguments by evolutionists.

1. Arbitrariness
   a. Mere opinion (opinion without justification)
   b. Relativism (no absolutes, and truth is subjective)
   c. Prejudicial conjecture (substitutes for knowledge)
   d. Unargued philosophical bias (our bias slants our interpretation of evidence because we have a worldview)

2. Inconsistency
   a. Logical fallacies
   b. *Reductio ad absurdum* ("reducing to absurdity")
   c. Behavioral inconsistency (action speaks louder than words)
   d. Presuppositional tensions (secular presuppositions are self-refuting)

3. Preconditions of Intelligibility
   a. Laws of logic
   b. Uniformity of nature
   c. Morality
   d. The basic reliability of our senses (see, hear, taste, smell, touch)
   e. The basic reliability of our memory
   f. Personal dignity and freedom

It is not our purpose to discuss these three requirements and all the criticisms that Lisle describes. Suffice it to say that Lisle criticizes evolutionists extensively based on these points.[49]

While Lisle may conclude that everybody has a worldview, that conclusion does not necessarily make it a fact. He argues that a worldview must be consistent. All Christians do not believe in one "Christian" worldview which violates the requirement that Lisle specifies. It is true that Christians have various basic beliefs, biases, and knowledge, but all Christians do not have all the same basic beliefs, biases, or the same knowledge. Even their theology varies because there are numerous Christian denominations. One denomination, for example, may believe that communion represents the actual body and blood of Christ while others believe communion represents the symbol of the body and blood of Christ. Some Christians even believe they should use grape juice instead of wine as the symbol of Christ's blood. Some Christians believe in the adoration of Mary, the mother of Jesus, while others abhor any such adoration. Some Christians believe they should not eat meat on Friday while others have no such belief. Because there are numerous denominations who call themselves Christian, as a consequence, there are numerous differences among Christians, each denomination with some different beliefs.

Evolutionists likewise have various basic beliefs, biases, and knowledge. Lisle even points out that some evolutionists believe in naturalism, a belief that nature is all there is. Other evolutionists believe in empiricism, a belief that all knowledge is gained from observations. A similar variety of thinking exists among other people, including people of different religions and those scientists who live in different parts of the world. There are probably as many beliefs, biases, and knowledge as there are people on earth. That also means there are likewise many worldviews if we accept Lisle's point of view that people have worldviews. This means that every person is a different collection of beliefs, prejudices, assumptions, and knowledge. That does not mean that there can't be common beliefs among groups of people. Indeed, that occurs, for sure. Nevertheless, there is not enough consensus and consistency among Christians or other groups that Lisle insists on to justify calling their beliefs a "Christian worldview." So, the bottom line is that a Christian worldview is not monolithic or necessarily widely held among all Christians, let alone among other groups of people. And there is a similar variety in other groups as well.

Another issue that Dr. Lisle brings up is the question of an ultimate standard. He categorically says that creationists "embrace the Bible as our ultimate standard."[50] He blatantly claims, *"The ultimate proof of creation is this: if biblical creation were not true, we could not know anything* [Italics from Lisle]*!"*[51] "This proof can be stated in a number of different ways, but what it really comes down to is this: *only the Christian worldview* (starting with a literal Genesis) *can rationally make sense of the universe*. Only if biblical creation is true can we have genuine knowledge about anything [emphasis mine]."[52] Otherwise, people's views are irrational. He directly says, "The Bible must be the ultimate standard because no other standard can make knowledge possible."[53] This is so obviously false that it must be dismissed as false.

The third of the three issues involve discrepancies in the Bible. It is clear that the New Testament, as we know it, was written and developed during the first four centuries after Christ as a way to create a unified Christian message to attract more followers. Numerous sects, including the Essenes, the Gnostics, and many other emerging sections propagated their own version of religious thought that competed with the Christian, Jewish, and pagan ways of thinking. However, over the years, people became aware of numerous contradictions between the four Gospels that became the foundation of Christianity and part of the New Testament. The four Gospels are Matthew, Mark, Luke, and John. They tell us about the life and work of Jesus Christ.

According to critics, each Gospel contains a mix of fact, rumor, legend, and myth that had gone through numerous translations, edits, and redactions. While the Old Testament was written in Hebrew, the New Testament was written in Greek. Matthew and Luke recount the temptation of Christ in the wilderness, but Jesus was alone when that happened. It is also true of Jesus when he prayed in the Garden of Gethsemane. Luke wrote that Jesus offered his prayer in Gethsemane "*a stone's throw away.*" When Jesus returned, he found the disciples asleep, was promptly arrested, and then led away for his crucifixion. There's no mention of Jesus ever saying a word to explain his prayer in the garden or the temptation in the wilderness. Nevertheless, we know all about the two events. How is that possible? One logical answer is the Gospel is not a word-for-word transcript of the events (before, during, or after). It would be a simple matter for Jesus to tell his disciples all about the two events. It is simply not recorded. How is that not obvious?

Another complaint is that all the Gospels describe the disciples fleeing when Jesus was arrested. So, if none of the Gospel authors were there, how can the Gospels provide a detailed account of the crucifixion? We know that the Mother of Jesus was in fact there at the crucifixion. She probably described what happened. If Christ was resurrected, he, too, could have described about what happened. Since we don't possess actual transcripts or movies of his appearances before the disciples, how can we summarily dismiss such possibilities? It is terribly easy to doubt but more difficult to believe in true possibilities. It's been said that some individuals may believe they will succeed in life while others believe they will fail. Both groups are right. Our thinking produces the result we choose to believe. The same phenomenon exists when we discuss the New Testament.

The greatest inconsistencies, some say, exist in the four Gospels' description of the crucifixion. The Gospels don't even agree on the date.

John said it was the day before Passover while the other three asserted it was the day after. Supposedly, even Jesus' final words varied among the Gospels. Matthew and Mark claimed it was, "My God, my God. Why have you forsaken me?"

Luke wrote, "Father, into your hands I commit my spirit."

And John offered simply, "It is finished." These Gospel writers wrote their four Gospels over a period of 400 years. Is it possible that they each emphasized points they thought were important? Since again no transcripts were made, is it possible that all those final words of Christ were spoken? Since we were not there, how can we definitively question what Jesus said? If someone were to line up ten people in line and whisper something into the ear of the first person at one end of the line, and every person in turn would whisper what he or she heard to the next person in line, what would be the result when the last person announced what he or she was told? We know it would be totally different than the original comment offered to the first person in line. Another example is to hear the testimony of six witnesses standing on the four corners of an intersection after they witnessed a car accident involving two cars. The same phenomenon would apply as in the witnesses hearing the final words of Christ. One person would hear some of what Jesus said, and others would hear different things. Again, we don't have a transcript. As we see in the two examples, different people have different perspectives of what they see and/or hear. We simply have the perceptions of some people but not a full accurate perception of any one person.

Furthermore, since the Gospels were written over a long period of time, it is likely that the description of events were passed down from one person to another and from one generation to another generation. So, some things could have been forgotten and some things could have been added to the description during the course of time. The same phenomenon that can occur with a line of ten people in line would also apply over time and over generation after generation. So, these and other apparent contradictions may have simple, logical explanations when one thinks about what happened and the time during which it happened. There is no doubt that scholars who have studied the Bible more extensively can present more contradictions and conflicts in the Bible than are more simply presented here. It is only our intent to demonstrate a preliminary introduction to the subject. In spite of all the variations, the Bible states that it—the Bible—can be used for reproof and correction. This means that it is valid enough to be authoritative for Christians.

One could ask hundreds of other questions about why God did something or failed to do something that we humans presume to suppose that He needed to do from our limited, myopic perspective. We neglect to see a bigger picture from God's perspective and insight. While we may not be satisfied with God and His action or inaction, life and existence do not depend on us. Instead, those things depend on God, for better or for worse. One would think that humans would judge God less and give him more credit for what He has accomplished and knowing what to do, how, and when.

We finished talking about three related issues, namely major calamities in history, some basic interpretations of creation and science, plus some inconsistencies in the Bible that critics bring up when discussing the Bible. Now that we have examined a lot of evidence, what can we conclude from this research? We will discuss this in the next chapter.

CHAPTER 10

Conclusion

The purpose of this exploration and analysis was to determine whether or not God exists. Can we verify or prove that God exists? It is time to present our conclusion. There are several issues to examine. First, we will look at a key point about scientific "facts." Secondly, we will look at a fundamental point about how life is directed or non-directed. Then we will review various sciences, plus mathematics and laws of science. Next, we will remind the reader about the Big Bang Theory, which purports to explain creation. Subsequently, we will cover the concept of a worldview and the ultimate standard and how they are used to justify the Biblical point of view. Finally, we will finish our conclusion.

Some scientists, like Stephen Hawking and Paul Davies, assert that God does not exist. However, they make circuitous claims based on limited evidence and conclusions, and they neglect to conduct a full, thorough examination of the basic question we stated above. History is replete with scientific "facts" that eventually have been proven to be false or incorrect, to say the least. The lesson we need to learn from these changes of scientific facts through history is that scientists are growing in their thinking and developing more knowledge over time. Those that precipitously jump to conclusions without thorough investigation and analysis of solid evidence actually need to find better evidence that actually supports or contradicts the existence of God instead of making those assumptions or jumping to conclusions that God does not exist or arbitrarily deciding that God must exist in some form that they deem appropriate. They cannot merely assume one position or the other. As I see it, scientists tend to look at their own scientific work, examine a few facts with blinders on, and arbitrarily conclude that there is no God. Either side cannot select only the facts that support their own prejudices. They need to examine the evidence on both sides of the issue. If they make the effort to gather all the evidence and analyze it better, they are more likely to find out the truth.

So, let us continue our discussion about a fundamental point as we move to start to answer our basic question. As previously discussed, all human, animal, and plant life must be either directed or non-directed. There can be no other alternative. The evidence very clearly demonstrates that all life is directed. Human, plant, and animal life reproduce after its own kind. Humans reproduce humans. Plant life reproduces the same kind of plants like the original plant. Also, animals reproduce their own kind. What's more we have seen that both plant and animal life are extremely organized in numerous levels of organization that cannot occur by random or accidental occurrences, even over extreme lengths of time at that level of precision. Does it make logical sense to assume that plant life would accidentally or by random divide itself into seven or more levels of solid organization? Does it make sense to assume that random events or accidents caused all the levels of organization of animal life? Certainly not.

When we examined the human anatomy, we found enormous complexity in the human body. The eye, brain, and liver serve as examples of some of the intricate, complex organs to demonstrate this point. The brain has a hundred billion neurons. Does that happen by accident, by chance, or by design? The retina of the eye contains 137 million light-sensitive cells. How does that happen? "The millions of specialized cells in your eye can analyze more than one million messages a second and then transmit the data to the brain," said Grant Jeffrey. How do we explain such incredible activity? The heart and other organs reveal similar complexity and intricacy and further document this observation. Looking at astronomy, we found an enormous universe with billions of stars in every galaxy and billions of galaxies in the universe that has a very specific and intricate organization. We look at all the constellations in the earth's sky as one sign of that. That obviates their creation by accident or random events, even through millions of years. While it is clear that there is still so much to learn about the universe, there is enough evidence to clearly show that the universe is too vast with its own complexity and organization to have developed by accident or by random events. All these areas of science demonstrate regularity, order, coordination, and direction which demonstrate signs of creation by a superior intelligent being.

When we looked at mathematics, we saw coordination, order, uniformity in the various branches of mathematics, including arithmetic, algebra, geometry, and calculus. Through my actual experience in my own studies of math up through calculus, I found that there are very specific ways to make simple and sophisticated calculations that we use to determine results that we can apply to various areas of life. There is frequently more than one way to calculate the same results. This means we can apply the different methods and disciplines in those different branches of mathematics. This kind of methodology and process demonstrates planning and organization in these disciplines by some kind of intelligent being. These forms of mathematics did not just happen out of the blue because some random or accidental events, like the creation of planets, had nothing better to do than to create mathematics. As I previously said, these kind of calculations demonstrate advanced planning and purpose by a higher intelligence or being.

Next, we checked out chemistry and physics and found again disciplines that are quite well organized. Examples of organization of chemistry are its Periodic Table of elements and the different areas of study in physical chemistry, organic chemistry, and inorganic chemistry. Physics is a fundamental branch of science but has become so complex and extensive with classical mechanics, quantum theory, and the theory of relativity. Both chemistry and physics have laws of science that control so many events that happen in our world and in our universe. We presented law after law in both chemistry and physics to demonstrate the orderliness of these sciences. There are so many laws that the allegation of repeated accidents or random activity cannot adequately explain or justify, even the existence of those laws of science, let alone create the laws they explain or to which they apply.

The Scientific Method is an orderly way to discover the truth about an issue under question. Stephen Hawking clearly pointed out that one can disprove a theory being offered as a law of science by finding just a single observation that disagrees with the thesis. A law of science must be true at all times and in all experiments. As we previously cited, Hawking said, "The whole history of science has been the gradual realization that events do not happen in an arbitrary manner but that they reflect a certain underlying order…" In spite of Hawking later declaring there is no god, nevertheless, he made a very profound and *accurate* statement. Note that he stated there is a "gradual realization." The development of science has been slow and gradual over the centuries. Since there is such order, it strongly suggests that Hawking's statement is at least a tacit admission of a higher intelligence as its source.

Since there are so many laws of science that govern so many things in existence, we need to ask an important question. Where did all those laws such as those we cited earlier come from? Don't those laws indicate definitiveness? Don't those laws demonstrate order? Do those laws happen by accident? By random action? Hardly. They must have come from a higher intelligence or being. It is too much to conclude erroneously that they all resulted from periodic accidents or random events over time. The very existence of the laws provides evidence of the Creator. The laws have no power or ability in themselves to create anything, as some "scientists" purport. The laws merely describe how things behave in certain circumstances. If it weren't for those laws of science, science would develop haphazardly and without uniform direction. Thus, there is a guiding hand to cause the direction science moves.

Stephen Hawking and Paul Davies were two of the leading scientists who proclaimed The Big Bang Theory to describe how the universe began. In others words, creation. They explained how a glob of material started with a very high density under a very high temperature and then expanded to the extent it has to now. They confess that they cannot identify the exact moment of creation. Since they did not observe that moment and have no practical evidence of it, they can only guess what happened and can only approximate when it happened. So, it is possible that their description may be true, and it is possible that there may be another explanation of creation. However, they cannot identify any source for this process of creation. They cannot legitimately say it is God, and they cannot legitimately say it is *not* God. They simply don't know. They are apparently afraid to concede that they don't know and leave it for future scientists to examine the evidence and find the truth. Furthermore, their claims merely describe a process but fail to describe or even ascertain the actual, exact cause of the process. They have not researched the subject scientifically nor conducted a full examination of all the evidence in order to reach a valid *scientific* conclusion. Statements that those scientists make are frequently prejudicial, characterizations, and assumptions, plus without deep study or adequate consideration of significant evidence. Paul Davies describes three possible theories for creation, including chemical self-assembly, microbes traveling through space, and life starting deeply within the earth. He fails to describe the root cause for those three actions or events. He also talks about DNA but fails to ascertain how DNA was created. No rational explanation is offered. If he cannot offer a reasonable explanation for the precise cause of any of his theories of creation, why should we believe any of his theories?

In addition, they cannot explain clearly how other galaxies and planets were formed. They offered ideas but offer little concrete proof for them. Since they cannot recreate the creation, they have no way of providing proof of creation. Apparently, the best way that they can offer evidence for the creation of earth is to observe the creation of stars from which they deduce how earth and the Milky Way galaxy were created. While that procedure may offer some insight into creation, it in itself does not constitute actual proof of creation to the exclusion of all other possibilities. However, they do have the means to measure the expansion of the universe to a reasonable degree. So, that part is provable. And it seems that they are correct in describing that process.

Dr. Sjoerd L. Bonting offered his novel "*creatio ex nihilo*" theory about the origin of the universe. Most scientists do not necessarily agree with his theory. However, he added some important ideas to the discussion. The main point that I learned was his idea that God is still creating since His initial creation activity of six "days." As just mentioned, the universe continues to expand. Stars are dying and turning into black holes or quasars. Some animals are becoming extinct. Changes are occurring on our earth and throughout the universe. So, it is not hard to believe that Bonting may be right about God creating on a continuous basis since the day He rested.

Let's turn our attention to a Christian perspective, in particular, from Dr. Jason Lisle. To remind the reader, Lisle claims everybody has a worldview through which they interpret evidence. He points out that creationists and evolutionists have the "same evidence," but both groups reach "different conclusions" from the evidence because of their different worldviews. He compares the two groups and claims the Christian worldview offers a more sensible way to explain scientific reasoning, logical deductions, morality, and other things.[54]

My conclusion is that Lisle's assumption that everybody has a worldview is fallacious. Earlier I pointed out that Christians do not have a uniform worldview because of all the different Christian denominations and their different beliefs. Evolutionists also have different basic beliefs, including naturalism versus empiricism. Lisle's belief in a worldview does not constitute proof, at least in accordance with the scientific method. The scientific method allows scientists to test and retest theories that never have any exceptions. A retest must yield the same result, as previously noted by Stephen Hawkins (see Chapter 4 where Hawking describes how to disprove a theory). Lisle sets up a strawman's argument to prevent contradictions to his theory. The fact that other people do not believe in his prejudices about what he calls his worldview constitutes proof that his worldview is fallacious and total nonsense.

Prior to the Bible, Egyptians built great pyramids, as did the Incas in Peru and the Aztecs in Mexico. They were very rational in how they built those great works. The Chinese also had great civilizations for centuries before the Bible was written. The concepts of rationality and uniformity existed in those civilizations on three different continents. Lisle's theory fails scientific testing. However, Lisle does present a comprehensive, indeed thorough, presentation of assumptions that creationists and evolutionists make when discussing their points of view. Lisle offers some clear examples of how evolutionists erroneously commit these fallacies. What Lisle needs to do is to subject creationists to this same type of thorough examination and analysis. If he or someone else would do that analysis, it would not be hard to conclude that creationists commit the same mistakes evolutionists commit as a result.

Lisle basically invents the concept of worldview, so that he can use that to defend his theory that the Bible is the only truth that humans can rely on. It appears that Lisle tries to preclude valid counter arguments. Lisle states categorically, "The argument is that the Bible's account of origins (along with its other accounts) must be *true* [emphasis mine]."[55] Like his other statements, this statement is very arbitrary and fallacious at its extreme. Lisle violates his own "sins" of arbitrariness and preconditions of intelligibility, as well as his thorough descriptions of the fallacies of ambiguity and fallacies of presumption that are outlined above. His assertions about the validity of the Christian worldview are without real evidence of their truthfulness, but his criticisms of the arguments by evolutionists are significantly accurate, as far as they go. He fails to see the validity of arguments presented by evolutionists. Also, he fails to examine the fallacies of the Christian "worldview."

The Bible is the inspired word of God, as Christians claim. It was written by human beings who received inspiration and spiritual guidance from

God. While the Bible has contradictions and deviations among its books, it is still a sacred work from God. It is striking how accurate it is in its descriptions of history. Who created science? God. Indeed, God created the universe and all that is in it and the earth and all that is on it. Since God created both the Bible and science, I argue that both the Bible and science say the same thing. God does not lie or tell false-hoods. There is no actual contradictions between the two—science and the Bible. Since humankind perceives that there are contradictions be-tween the two arguments, that means those apparent contradictions are the result of misinterpretations of the Bible, of science, and/or of both the Bible and science. Since so many people, including scientists, priests, pastors, educated scholars, and normal people, misinterpret the Bible and/or science, it causes tremendous uncertainty, confusion, and misinformation to many people who want to make sense of things.

One example is the story of creation. The Bible says that God created the universe and the earth in six days and rested on the seventh day. Many Christians assume that the Bible means seven days with twenty-four hours each, as we humans measure time. Thanks to Dr. Jason Lisle for this quote from Isaiah 55:8-9: "For my thoughts are not your thoughts, neither are your ways my ways, declares the Lord. As the heavens are higher than the earth, so are my ways higher than your ways and my thoughts than your thoughts."[56] This passage very clearly states that human beings do not think like God thinks, and human be-ings do not act in the same way as God acts. How can any Christian as-sume that God must be as limited in time as a human being to twenty-four hours in a day? Is God not greater in size and power than a human? Furthermore, the Bible says that a day for God is like a thou-sand years for a human. If God is the Creator, then the sense of time cannot be equal for God and humankind. It must be different for God and for humans. So, it necessarily follows that the time perspective of

God is significantly greater than that of humans. So, a statement from the Bible that a "flick of the eye" or a "day" to God represents a thousand years to a human is a reasonable statement and is probably true. Christians proclaim that the Bible is the word of God. In the Bible, according to Isaiah 55:8-9, God states clearly that His ways are greater than those of a human, and His thoughts are higher than those of a human. So, if these two passages from the Bible are true, that clearly shows how God could have taken millions of years to carry out His creation instead of doing it in "several thousand years," as some Christians falsely presume. We have already seen that adding up the life times of people listed in the Bible from Adam and Eve up to Noah was more than 10,000 years, which by itself negates the theory that the age of the earth is merely "several thousand years [as Lisle mistakenly claims]." If a Christian truly believes in God, he or she must admit that God is not a genie that can be put into a bottle of one day of a human's twenty-four hours timetable. How can we try to limit God, the Creator of the entire universe with billions of galaxies, each of which has billions of stars and planets, into a small human—sized mind or frame? It's like putting the Creator of the whole universe into a grain of sand on the Malibu beach in California. It is too fallacious to contemplate.

While we did not examine the earth per se, it is abundantly clear from normal observation that the seas, rivers, and oceans are useful to humanity in numerous ways, beautiful, bountiful to see, and beneficial to the environment. The same is true of plants, flowers, animals, insects, and all creatures on the earth. Some scientists would claim that the planets in the solar system have useful purposes for the benefit of the earth and its people. As an example, the planet Jupiter may provide significant protection of the earth from numerous meteorites from space. The moon affects the rise and fall of the tides of the oceans. If the moon were not at the precise distance from the earth that it is, it would cause major repercussions on the earth. According to Wikipedia, the earth consistently rotates around the sun 584 million miles for 365.256 days at an average distance of 92.96 million miles. The time over 365 days is accounted for by the leap years in our calendars. If the earth did not rotate on its axis and spin around the sun as it does, the earth could collapse from its path and end all life on earth, according to scientists. These observations constitute more evidence that proves the existence of the Creator. A deeper exploration of these facts will provide additional support for the conclusion of this book.

God has a great sense of humor. His irony is truly incredible. It is astonishing that all human senses—sight, hearing, smell, taste, and touch—in their own way confirm the beauty and wonder of creation by an intelligent being. The beauty of flowers, the sound of music or people talking, the smell of food being cooked or served at a dinner table, the taste of meals, wine, beer, or other things, and the touch of another person all make us aware of the wonder around each of us. While we may take these things for granted, each in their own way are confirmations of God's existence.

In spite of the fear and outright refusal of some "scientists" to admit it, God created all plant, animal, and human life, science, mathematics, and progress in all areas. I have endeavored to provide a reasonable explanation and evidence of my points. I hope this helps people to better understand God and how He works in the world, and indeed, in the universe. I cannot offer a complete explanation at this point in time because of my ignorance. Perhaps over time, others will be able to add to this story and offer additional information and understanding.

After completion of this examination and analysis, the conclusion of this study is that science proves the existence of God. Sir Arthur Conan Doyle wrote the books about the great detective Sherlock Holmes. In those stories, the great detective would go to a crime scene and notice the numerous clues and significantly deduce some key facts about the crime. For example, Holmes would find a used cigarette in an ash tray with lipstick on it and would realize that the murder victim had been killed by a woman or she was a witness to the crime. Holmes would deduce that the killer or the victim was a smoker. The evidence that was previously cited clearly demonstrates that God exists and created the universe, earth, science, and all the signs that show direction and purpose. We see actual evidence, and we deduce facts from the evidence we have. All the evidence demonstrates intent, direction, organization, and even focus that clearly that can only come from a Creator, or in other words, God.

To date, while scientists have offered numerous theories to explain creation, their theories basically boil down to three fundamental theories to explain the creation of the universe, the solar system and human, animal, and plant life. Those three theories explain creation by accident, by random, or by God. The numerous theories offered come down to basically one of these three alternatives. No scientist nor anyone else has offered any other rational, realistic theory to explain creation. If creation occurred by accident, then various freak or other kinds of accidents would have occurred and caused various deviations in its results in every aspect of life, solar system, and the universe. Creation by accident would not have created such order or such consistency throughout the universe, solar system, or life. That explanation would allow deviations or mutations in human, animal, and plant life that do not really exist. If creation occurred by random, then it would be even clearer that deviations and mutations would exist in every aspect of existence. There would be no limitations in any kind of growth or change, as was explained earlier in this study. For example, you would see many humans with three arms, four legs, or numerous other mutations and deviations. Animals would deviate similarly. Plants would vary also. It is unequivocally clear that creation by random or by accident would deviate in numerous and various ways and would never develop real order or consistency in its changes. Those alternative theories could never develop the extensive organization, for example, that exists in botany or zoology, as previously discussed. Those theories could never develop the incredible order and consistency found in human beings. Those theories are merely guesses and fail to describe the basic, or root, cause for the universe. The scientists weren't there to observe and measure the creation of the universe. They cannot replicate the creation of another universe equal in size and scope as the current universe.

There is only one theory that fully explains creation, that is, the fact that God is the Creator. Scientists who deny this fact have no reasonable evidence to the contrary and merely rely on their prejudice and their foolish desire to deny the existence of God. For example, Stephen Hawking's conclusion that there is no God relies less on actual science and more on his anger and frustration with his physical handicaps, which were very significant. Scientists have not seriously conducted actual investigations of evidence about whether or not a supreme being created the universe, the planets, and the laws of science, human beings, animals, or plants. Their conclusions about the existence of God are usually by-products of their studies about the creation process of the earth. They endeavor more to describe the steps as opposed to explaining the source of those steps. Those scientists who deny the existence of God ignore the basics of science and fail to explain the basics facts and examples cited in this study.

I have presented a considerable amount of evidence to support the thesis of this work, but the evidence presented is but the tip of the iceberg, so to speak. While I cited a few sciences as examples of my evidence, there are many other sciences that also support my thesis. The evidence is actually substantial and overwhelming. The purpose of this study was to review some significant works instead of being an exhaustive work that examined every work or every science in detail and in depth. In addition, as time goes on, more and more evidence will be uncovered to provide more powerful proof. This is only the beginning. The bottom line is this: If what I wrote is false, no amount of assertion by me will make it true. However, if what I wrote is true, no amount of denial by others will make it false. We all have to contend with that fact.

This study was not about an examination of the divinity of Jesus Christ, the doctrine of Christianity, the different denominations, the differences between them including Catholicism, or anything to do with Christianity. Its sole purpose was to examine the evidence about the existence of God and reach a conclusion. This study concludes that science itself definitively proves the existence of God, the creator of the universe, the earth, and all animal, plant, and human life.

To close, I offer this following quotation from Job 38:1-7.

> Then the Lord answered Job out of the storm. He said:
>
> Who is this that darkens my counsel with words without knowledge? Brace yourself like a man: I will question you, and you shall answer me.
>
> Where were you when I laid the earth's foundation? Tell me if you understand.

Who marked off its dimensions? Surely, you know!
Who stretched a measuring line across it?

On what were its footings set, or who laid its corner-
stone—while the morning stars sang together and all
the angels shouted for joy?

Read verses 8-29 for the rest of the quotation used in this chapter. Read
Chapters 39 to 42 to read the full quotation from *The Student Bible*,
New International Version, (Grand Rapids, MI: Zondervan Bible Pub-
lishers, 1984), pp. 481-482.

AFTERWORD

Now that we know that God exists and is the creator of the universe including all planets, things, animals, and humans, what does that mean for humans? That is probably the question that comes to mind for most people. So, let's explore a few brief thoughts.

First, since God created billions of planets in our galaxy and billions of galaxies in our universe, it seems there is a high probability of life on other planets. That does not necessarily mean that life on other planets is the same kind of life as humans on earth. According to Wikipedia, the chemical composition of the air that surrounds the earth consists of 78.09% nitrogen, 20.95% oxygen, 0.93% argon, 0.04% carbon dioxide, and small quantities of other gases. Air is retained around the earth by gravity. Other beings may exist on other planets in other galaxies and may exist in similar and/or different environments. The composition of "air" on other planets may have different quantities of nitrogen, oxygen, and carbon dioxide for example. Maybe another planet may have 50% nitrogen, 25% oxygen, 10% argon, and 10% carbon dioxide, plus other gases. Or perhaps that planet may have 70% nitrogen, 10% oxygen, 15% argon, and 20% carbon dioxide. Perhaps the creatures inhabiting the planet will have different breathing mechanisms in their bodies than humans. Maybe some beings will be more intelligent than humans while others may be less intelligent. In other words, other beings could have many different characteristics than humans on earth have. There is no law in the universe that compels all creatures to exist, live, look, or breathe like humans on earth.

Secondly, humans have evolved and developed over time as we previously described. That means humans are getting more knowledgeable, sophisticated, and hopefully wiser. This growth and development has been guided by God. We do not know to what extent His guidance or direction has influenced human growth. On some planets, God may have significantly guided the growth and development of the inhabitants more than He guided humans on earth and may have guided the inhabitants less on other planets. While humans may have a huge amount of evolution and growth to go, humans are developing in many ways and in many areas of life. For example, humans are learning to control a country's economy more effectively through supply-side and demand-side economics.

Demand-side economists are frequently called Keynesian economists after John Maynard Keynes, who developed his economic theories principally in response to the Great Depression of the 1930's. They believe the demand for goods and services constitute the primary factor that causes economic activity and short-term fluctuations. Keynes claimed that unemployment resulted from an inadequate demand for goods. He saw idle factories, unemployed workers during the Great Depression due to insufficient demand for their products. Consequently, he claimed that factories did not have enough demand for workers. He thought that this lack of demand caused unemployment to continue, which meant the market was unable to correct itself and return to normal behavior. He called this a lack of aggregate demand, a core principle of demand-side economics. According to Keynes, aggregate demand consisted of four elements. These were as follows:

1. Consumption of goods and services
2. Investment by industry in capital goods
3. Government spending on public goods
4. Net exports.

Keynes advocated that the government should spend money to help overcome low aggregate demand in the short-term, such as during a recession or depression, to lower unemployment and to stimulate growth in the economy. John F. Kennedy in the early 1960's provided an example of using Keynesian economics to guide the American economy. He got Congress to approve significant tax cuts for Americans and increased government spending. As a result, the U. S. economy grew and prospered. His actions provided an important lesson for leaders on how to grow the economy.

Supply-side economists assert that increased production promotes economic growth. The factors of production are capital, labor, entrepreneurship, and land. So, supply-side economists believe that fiscal policy will create a better climate for business with its use of tax cuts and deregulation. When companies benefit from these policies, those companies are able to hire more workers. As a consequence, that job growth creates more demand, which also boosts the economy. When the companies are given incentives to expand through deregulation and removal of restrictions on their growth that lowers the costs for operating their businesses and even enables them to expand into new areas. A corporate tax cut gives businesses more money to hire workers, invest in capital equipment, and produce more goods and services. There are different times when one theory of economics has been more effective than the other. It is not the purpose of this study to delve deeply into this subject. The point of this discussion is to say that humans are getting more and more sophisticated in their knowledge and ability to manage a country's economy through more effectively utilizing these economic tools at different key times. However, it is necessary to recognize that this knowledge is just beginning to be understood and used properly.

Ronald Reagan in the 1980's provided an example of using supply-side economics to guide the American economy with his different approach. He got Congress to approve significant tax cuts for Americans and reduced regulations. As a result, the U. S. economy again grew and prospered. Two different approaches showed leaders and economists how both approaches improved the economy. The question is which approach needs to be applied in which circumstances. This is an area in which economists have room to learn more. Since humans have been growing and since creation, humans are developing in knowledge and ability to do things that centuries ago were barely dreams.

It is quite possible, and probably likely, that humankind will continue to develop and become smarter, wiser, and more sophisticated over the centuries. Eventually, humans will begin to understand God more clearly and definitively as time moves on. I suggest that at some point, humankind will understand God pretty well. At that point in time, Jesus will come again, as the Bible predicted. It could actually take thousands of years before that happens. If one reads the signs in the Bible that indicate Jesus will come again, it probably describes every year that humans live. So, it confuses humans and makes some people think that it will never happen—which is what God expects. If the Bible suggests that a flick of the eye is a thousand years to God's frame of reference, it seems unlikely that God would send His only son to return to earth after a few thousand years. That doesn't seem realistic or practical, from God's point of view, I would suggest. On the other hand, one probably and logically questions whether God would wait as long as 10,000 years before having Jesus return. Of course, that kind of thinking is the way humans think instead of the way God thinks. So, will Jesus return sooner or later? All we know is that it will be totally without warning and unexpected.

These are some thoughts about the meaning of God's existence for humankind. Their purpose is to encourage people to think more about God and His will and how His will may be different for other living beings. If people start to think more as God thinks, they will grow in wisdom and knowledge, I submit.

ACKNOWLEDGMENTS

Supporting this author is a talented team of creative professional individuals. I want to acknowledge both the unsung experts and the ones with which I directly worked at Dorrance Publishing Company. They all helped me through the various steps of the publishing process including copy editing, page design, cover design, page proofs, and illustrations creation. The periodic contacts from David Zeolla, President of Dorrance, were very much appreciated as we moved through the different steps. I want to acknowledge and thank Erin Serena, my Project Coordinator, for her patient caring and support through most of the publishing steps. A true professional. I particularly want to acknowledge and thank the cover designer Tess Kamban for the perfect cover design, the one that I envisioned as she did, like two minds acting as one. And I want to express my appreciation to Rachael Bindas for taking over the responsibility as Project Coordinator to handle the final steps of the publishing process. She is certainly a talented professional as well.

I am so grateful for this talented team for their support to try to fashion the best quality and professional book that we can produce. For everyone who reads and appreciates this book, it is due so much to this team's wonderful help and guidance.

Last but certainly not least, I want to thank my darling wife Marice for her loving patience and support through the writing and publishing of this book.

FOOTNOTES

1. Abraham H. Maslow. *Motivation and Personality* (New York: Harper, 1954), pp. 80-92.
2. Grant R. Jeffrey, *Creation: Remarkable Evidence of God's Design*, (New York: WaterBrook, 2003), p. 38.
3. Ibid, pp. 42-43.
4. Ibid, pp. 47-48.
5. *American Heritage Student Dictionary*, Second Edition, Copyright @ 2014 by Houghton Mifflin Harcourt Publishing Company.
6. Stephen Hawking, *A Brief History of Time*, (New York: Bantam Books, 2017), page 10.
7. Ibid, page 10.
8. Ibid, page 10.
9. Ibid, page 127.
10. Paul Davies, *The Mind of God*, (New York: Simon and Schuster Paperbacks, 1992), p. 84.
11. Ibid, p. 81.
12. Ibid, p. 61.

13. Sjoerd L. Bonting, *Chaos Theology: A Revised Creation Theololgy* (Ottawa, Canada: Novallis, Saint Paul University, 2002), pp. 14-15.
14. Ibid, p. 20.
15. Ibid, pp. 21 and 27.
16. Ibid, p. 22.
17. Ibid, p. 25.
18. Paul Davies, *The 5th Miracle*, (New York: Simon & Schuster Paperbacks, 1999), p.17.
19. Ibid, p. 20.
20. Ibid, pp. 33-34.
21. Ibid, p. 41.
22. Ibid, p. 78.
23. Ibid, p. 83.
24. Ibid, p.138.
25. Ibid, pp.140-141.
26. Ibid, p. 141.
27. Ibid, p. 183.
28. Ibid, p. 183.
29. Ibid, p. 193.
30. Ibid, p. 201.
31. Ibid, p. 264.
32. Ibid, pp. 265-269.
33. Ibid, pp. 269-270.
34. *The Holy Bible*, New Revised Standard Version (New York; Oxford University Press, 1977), pp. 1-2.
35. Ibid.
36. Ibid.
37. Grant R. Jeffrey, *CREATION: Remarkable Evidence of God's Design*, (New York, WaterBrook Press, 2003), pp. 11-12.
38. Ibid, p.16.

39. Worthing, Mark William, *God, Creation, and Contemporary Physics*, (Minneapolis: Fortress Press, 1996), p. 4.

40. Ibid, p. 5.

41. Ibid, pp. 34-35.

42. Ibid, p. 105.

43. Ibid, p. 107.

44. Ibid, p. 132.

45. Ibid, pp. 134-137.

46. Paul Davies, *The Mind of God*, (New York: Simon and Schuster Paperbacks, 1992), p. 84.

47. Ibid, p. 81.

48. Lisle, Jason, *The Ultimate Proof of Creation*, (Green Forest, AR: Master Brooks, 2009), pp. 81-82.

49. Ibid, pp. 84-95.

50. Ibid, p.83.

51. Ibid, p. 40.

52. Ibid, p. 40.

53. Ibid, p. 156.

54. Ibid, p. 249.

55. Ibid, p 40.

56. *The Student Bible*, New International Version, (Grand Rapids, Michigan: Zondervan Bible Publishers, 1990) p. 650; also Dr. Lisle, *Ultimate Proof*, pp. 208-209.

SELECTED BIBLIOGRAPHY

American Heritage Student Dictionary, Second Edition, Copyright @ 2014 by Houghton Mifflin Harcourt Publishing Company.

Bonting, Sjoerd L., *Chaos Theology: A Revised Creation Theololgy* (Ottawa, Canada: Novallis, Saint Paul University, 2002)

Davies, Paul, *The 5th Miracle: The Search for the Origin and Meaning of Life* (New York: Simon & Schuster Paperbacks, 1999)

Davies, Paul, *The Mind of God: The Scientific Basis for a Rational World* (New York: Simon and Schuster Paperbacks, 1992)

Hawking, Stephen, *A Brief History of Time*, (New York: Bantam Books, 2017)

The Holy Bible, New Revised Standard Version (New York; Oxford University Press, 1977)